SALES
MASTERCLASS

SALES MASTERCLASS

80

ESSENTIAL TIPS AND TECHNIQUES FOR SERIOUS SALESPEOPLE

NIGEL HENZELL-THOMAS

Hutchinson
Business
Books

First published in Great Britain by
Hutchinson Business Books Limited
An imprint of Random Century Limited
20 Vauxhall Bridge Road, London SW1V 2SA

Random Century Australia (Pty) Limited
20 Alfred Street, Milsons Point
Sydney, NSW 2061, Australia

Random Century New Zealand Limited
9–11 Rothwell Avenue, Albany
Private Bag, North Shore Mail Centre
Glenfield, Auckland 10, New Zealand

Century Hutchinson South Africa (Pty) Limited
PO Box 337, Bergvlei 2012, South Africa

British Library Cataloguing in Publication Data
Henzell-Thomas, Nigel
Sales masterclass
1. Salesmanship
I. Title
658.8'5
ISBN 0-09-174381-8 (Pbk)
ISBN 0-09-174717-1

Typeset in Trump Mediaeval by ↗ Tek Art Ltd, Croydon, Surrey
Printed and bound in Great Britain by Mackays of Chatham PLC,
Chatham, Kent

Dedication

To Lu and Lucy for their continuing
patience and to Bob Usmar for his constructive
comments.

First Salesperson: I MANAGED TO MAKE
                        SOME VERY VALUABLE
                        CONTACTS TODAY.

Second Salesperson: I DIDN'T CLOSE ANY
                        ORDERS EITHER.

CONTENTS

Contents

Contents

Contents

I don't know who you are
I don't know your company
I don't know your company's product
I don't know what your company stands for
I don't know your company's customers
I don't know your company's record
I don't know your company's reputation
Now – what was it you wanted to sell me?

Source: by kind permission of
        McGraw Hill Inc

INTRODUCTION

In my first book, co-authored with David Peoples, *Supercharge Your Selling – 60 Tips in 60 Minutes*, the aim was to help you achieve incremental business, with much less effort, by making sure that you did all the right things the very first time. It consisted of useful and valid Tips and Techniques to ensure that you stayed in front of the selling game. It also demonstrated that selling, whilst being a serious business, should also be a business where an element of good natured humour exists.

Sales Masterclass is about successfully closing those bigger deals, where – in many skills areas – there are substantial differences in the attitudes and campaigns that must be adopted to be successful in closing the sale. In reality, of course, many of the Tips in *Supercharge* can equally apply to that bigger deal, but additional ideas and disciplines are the intention of this follow-on book. Should you not have read *Supercharge*, I would urge you to retain a copy.

If you think about it, you will realize that many facets of your life, and virtually all human success, is based, in part, on percentages. In many ways, your whole life revolves around percentages. In sport, for instance, what is it that separates a hero from a nobody? What is the difference between successful and unsuccessful tennis players? Probably that the successful tennis players achieve a higher percentage of 'aces' during their service games than the nobodys. In gambling, there are pros and amateurs. What's the difference? Most of the amateurs are on the slot machines. The professionals, on the other hand, mostly play blackjack, using Scarnes rules, where the percentages are most in their favour.

Percentages apply in selling too. Percentage selling is simply deciding where the highest percentage of success in your selling effort can be found and then using that percentage on a daily basis.

We all strive for those multiple sales (or those single large revenue items) with our prospect lists reflecting our aspirations in this area. No doubt you are striving to excel in your job, with your company also having certain expectations of you.

The search for that magic combination of traits that spells sure-fire sales ability in the environment of the bigger deal continues unabated. The number of lists that have been drawn up is countless. One observer, McMurry, listed five traits that he believed made a good salesperson. They were:

● A high energy level.
● Boundless self-confidence.
● A chronic hunger for money.
● A well-established habit for industry.
● A state of mind that regards each objection or obstacle as a challenge.

After several years of fieldwork, Mayer and Greenberg, writing in the *Harvard Business Review*, offered one of the shortest of lists of

Introduction

traits common to good salespeople ever written. They concluded that the good salesperson had two basic qualities: empathy – the ability to feel as the customer does; and ego-drive – a strong personal need to make the sale. An understanding of the following 'bottom-line' factors and associated attributes, will make you more successful than others in closing bigger deals:

● People buy from people they both like and trust.
● People like to buy, but they hate to be sold.
● People are complex and will eventually buy for a variety of reasons.
● Buying is a process of logical steps.

In this book I will concentrate on:

● Effective communication.
● Questioning.
● Handling objections.
● An effective 'practical selling cycle'.
● Account planning
● Presentation skills.
● Successful Seminars.

I have used the word 'salesperson' throughout the book, rather than 'account executive', 'consultant' or 'marketing representative'. A certain amount of pretension goes along with the last three. Good salespeople today are marketeers and possess exceptional skills in communication, including the ability to listen and question effectively, so that true prospect needs are drawn out and agreed. If you feel embarrassed by the word, then perhaps you are in the wrong profession!

The word 'solution' is used extensively, rather than 'product'. Today's salespeople are problem-solvers, and problem-solvers talk about solutions, not products.

I have also used the word 'prospect', rather than 'customer'. You will be approaching large accounts where you just do not have a presence, as well as meeting new people in existing accounts. So, in my view, everyone – through qualification – has a chance to become a true prospect. That is, a possible or likely new customer or a possible or likely extension of an existing relationship.

Whether you are a manager or not, in whichever company you work, performing whatever function, *never forget that you represent your company as a 'salesperson' in one guise or another.*

STEP ONE

THE BIG DEAL MEANS CHANGE

TIP *1* *Sell Change*

Depending on the circumstances, making large sales means you will need to apply a wide variety of knowledge and skills to any given sales situation. Fundamentally, you will need the ability to deal with the unexpected, to adjust to changing circumstances and to convince your customers and prospects to respond positively to your proposals. *You* must also learn to manage that change. This means developing your skills, capabilities and perceptions, which will make you stronger, more aware and more effective in your job.

To improve your skills, you must address the key areas as follows:

● **Learning.** To stay abreast of change, you must make learning a habit. Whether you are getting an update on your company's latest solutions and services or learning new sales techniques, you as an individual are constantly increas-ing your available knowledge and skills. Then learn to present any differences in terms of benefits to your prospects.

● **Leadership.** To effectively manage change, you must get personally involved, both as listener and communicator. Leadership doesn't mean being obviously ahead; it means positively making the way ahead clear.

● **Flexibility.** By keeping an open mind, you are more able to get to the core of a given situation. Maintaining that flexibility helps you to ask the right questions and get the information you need to make the right decisions.

● **Experience.** As you will deal with a variety of accounts, your experience is a key factor in all aspects of the change process. By involving yourself in different accounts, you increase your experience in making decisions quickly and efficiently.

● **Vision.** Having a proactive attitude about change means that you are constantly on the lookout for change opportunities within your large accounts. By consistently looking forward, you develop the attitude and the ability to anticipate possible future developments and to develop an account strategy in advance of change. Keeping an eye on the future is an effective way to avoid getting caught off-guard in the present.

The bottom line

Learning to recognize, understand, manage and sell change will make you a better listener and communicator, who knows how to get the best from key prospects: in short, a very successful salesperson.

TIP 2 *The Spin-Off*

Developing your skills in understanding, managing and selling change also has another benefit: it will strengthen your company. By improving the quality of interaction with your accounts, you improve the quality of interaction with your peers in the office, and with everyone you meet. Some of the ways in which it can benefit your company are:

● *Increased efficiency at work:* by implementing and testing new approaches to large account selling, not only you but also your colleagues can develop sales methods to save time and effort and accomplish more.
● *Increased marketplace response:* by keeping open to change, you can better meet your prospects' needs. As solutions and services come to the market, it is important to be able to identify and respond to your account's needs and requirements.
● *Being prepared for the future:* as your task is to sell change, you will demonstrate willingness and ability to look past the situations of today and imagine the challenges of the future. Others will be motivated by your example.

The bottom line
By developing these skills, not only will you increase sales by capitalizing on opportunities presented but also see opportunities to grow in your own company. Promotion comes natu-

rally to those who are seen as perceptive leaders!

STEP TWO

BE UNDERSTOOD
AT ALL LEVELS

Tip 3 Communicate Effectively

Successful communication is the only way to influence others. It is the purposeful and successful transfer of meaning between people. By the proper use of communication techniques in the environment of the bigger deal, you will influence people to take a desired course of action. You must be able to communicate effectively to succeed in your job and career in large account selling because:

- effective communication is the basis for selling; the forerunner of sales; the fundamental requirement necessary for all sales activity
- communication skills are useful within your own company, whether at secretarial, management or support level.

Successful communication is based on the understanding of the objectives of the prospects to whom you are talking. By communicating effectively, you will build trust and confidence with your customers, helping them to identify you as a highly-qualified individual and creating a favourable impression of your company. Most problems are not due to a solution or service deficiency, or even to people, but are a result of a breakdown in communication.

Bottom line
Relationships can fail through a lack of understanding. Successful salespeople must have

good relationships with their prospects. Relationships are based on effective communication, by thoughts, words and actions. Be sure that yours portray the right messages at all times.

TIP 4 A Good Communicator is a Good Person

Communication may seem rather simple, but it's actually an art which must be practised and perfected. Its success depends on your ability to maintain interest and to control the conversation. Always remember that a human being, not a company, makes the decision to buy. You have to maintain your *prospect*'s interest if you expect to achieve your objectives, and this involves all of the following qualities and techniques:

● *Be friendly, courteous and sincere:* treat your prospects on a person-to-person basis.
● *Use their name occasionally:* remember that the sweetest sound to a person is his or her own name, pronounced correctly.
● *Let them talk:* be alert and flexible, using your listening skills to determine what should be said next. Don't be impatient: they may have a message or problem to convey.
● *Think before you speak.*
● *Be positive:* a 'can do' attitude will keep your prospects tuned-in.
● *Speak in terms with which they are familiar:* avoid slang, buzz words, technical jargon or language that has no meaning for them. You can embarrass, confuse or anger people by using terms that they don't understand.
● *Different levels of management have different objectives, priorities and interests:* they speak different languages. *All* levels must believe you're the good guy.

- The final decision will be made at executive level and here, as at all the other levels, you must see their problems as they see them.
- Try to anticipate these thoughts and problems.
- Find out their points of view on what you're saying.
- Establish a common ground.
- Be a good conversationalist and don't interrogate.

● *Be concise:* don't waste time and confuse the issues with awkward phrases or badly-organized rambling.

  - Think carefully about what you are going to say.
  - Don't use 10 words when you can say it in three.
  - Don't try and impress your prospects with vocabulary. Use words that are simple and direct. Chose words that convey your exact thought.
  - Speak clearly. It may irritate your prospects if they must ask you to repeat what you've said.
  - Don't make your prospects search for meaning. They will lose interest.

● *Ask questions to maintain interest and keep the interview moving in the desired direction:* asking questions gives the other person a feeling of importance.

● *Know when to end a conversation:* if your

prospect keeps looking at his or her watch or showing other signs of disinterest, it's time to change or end your conversation. Leaving gracefully at these times is important in building a long-term relationship with prospects.

Bottom line
Good communication must be practised. It must also relate to the level of management you are dealing with, and to the circumstances. It's not easy, so practise!

TIP 5 The Importance of Listening

If there is a single stage that will make you sell bigger and better, it is that of listening. This will help you to avoid a breakdown in communications by allowing you to understand your prospects' objectives, and achieve those objectives, as well as your own.

Listening on a telephone is easier than listening to someone you can see: in the case of the former, all you can do is listen. Having all the clues that are available when you sit opposite your prospect makes listening very difficult, because in this situation you listen with your whole mind, not just your ears.

Most of us only go through the motions of listening . . . because we can hardly wait to get talking ourselves. Perhaps an initial comment your prospect makes triggers a bright response in your mind, or seems to provide the opportunity for you to meet one of your objectives for the meeting. You make intelligent-looking facial expressions until your prospect stops talking and then you start *telling* them things, instead of communicating. You may not realize that you are being a poor listener, but penalize yourself because you fail to absorb the information offered.

Bottom line
Listening is the single most important stage in large account selling.

TIP 6 Guidelines for Listening

Listening is difficult. Most people like to talk, but you can't listen while you are talking. Learn to stop talking. Listen and watch.

Listen for meaning. Your mind has the potential to process information at a much faster rate than you have the means to present it, so discipline in listening is needed. Concentrate on the important points, and summarize and repeat them in your mind as your prospect speaks to reinforce your understanding. Balance *what* was said and the *manner* in which it was said, to get the full meaning. Learn to listen for that meaning by asking yourself these questions:

● What did your prospect say?
● Is it fact or opinion?
● What did your prospect mean?
● Why did your prospect say it?
● Do you believe it?
● Does your prospect need the product?
● What is your prospect holding back? Why?
● Can your prospect's views be changed? How?
● Did you hear and understand your prospect's decision criteria?

Try to be aware of notable omissions: things *not said* can be just as informative as things said. Be aware of evasiveness.

Take notes as you listen: if you are listening properly, your prospects will be talking for the majority of the time and you may not remember all the opportunities that have been presented and which you can later explore. As well as helping you remember, note-taking shows your prospects that you attach some importance to what they are saying. Don't overdo notes, however, as this can alienate your prospects.

Bottom line

If you spot just one opportunity to tell your prospects about your company, solution and/or services – and you can't wait to speak – you haven't done enough listening. In the early stages of a campaign, the prospect should do most of the talking; your participation should be simply clarification, keeping the discussion on course and learning about their objectives and requirements.

Always verify that you have an accurate understanding of what was meant by repeating or rephrasing what you have heard or what you think you heard. Then ask your prospect to verify the accuracy of your understanding. This is especially important when the points being made by your prospect are those upon which you are going to take action. Some useful phrases to confirm significant issues are:

● If I understand you correctly . . .
● When you said . . .
● Am I right in assuming that this means . . .

Because you lose visual cues in telephone conversations, be particularly careful in listening over the telephone. When you can see your prospect, a significant topic can be recognized by:

● A change in gesture patterns (this usually requires time to identify a prospect's characteristic gestures)
● An abrupt change in posture
● An abrupt change of subject
● A more energetic participation in the conversation
● Withdrawal of eye contact.

Always be objective in your listening. Hear what the other person is saying, not just what you want to hear; not just what satisfies your specific objective for the call. Keep an open mind and be aware of your own enthusiasm, so as not to jump to conclusions.

Never react defensively. Don't visually or verbally over-react to what you hear, but ask for explanations of criticisms and concerns. Be aware of your own prejudices, and do not let these interfere with the purpose of your call.

For example, in the early stages of your campaign, do not let an apparent objection to doing business with your company involve you in a detailed discussion before you have finished listening. If your prospect's opening comments are, 'I don't intend to spend any more money in this area this year', don't say 'But our products (and/or services) can save you money'. This would introduce a cost-justification discussion before you have listened and understood where the opportunities really lie. The correct way to answer is, 'I understand that, but could you tell me how your company will develop in the future'.

Listening properly should demand your full concentration. Don't turn off your listening or let your attention wander. Your prospect may not be as good a communicator as you, so the burden of organizing and distilling their message falls to you. Try to shut out distractions, and listen for that real meaning.

Keep eye contact with your prospect. This will help you – and him or her – to remain involved. If you find yourself analyzing your prospect's clothes, delivery and looks, for example, you are not listening properly.

You may find, of course, that the prospect has wandered so far away from the issues concerned that your intervention is vital to bring him or her back to the subject. Some examples are:

● 'Good heavens, how surprising, but as you were saying earlier . . .'
● 'Yes, putting is the key to a low handicap. That's where most games are won or lost. You mentioned earlier that . . .'

TIP 7 *The Importance of Questioning*

To ensure that you understand exactly what you said, you must develop your skills in questioning – one of the most powerful communication skills available to you in sales at any level, and especially for bigger deals. Good questioning is essential to the discovery of need, the uncovering and clarification of objections and the gaining of agreement on proposed solutions. It is a conversational skill, not an interrogative device, and although Who, What, When, Where, Why and How are the starting points of effective questioning, the repetition of a phrase, such as 'Oh?', or even leaning forward and looking inquiringly, can be just as effective as a means of posing questions.

There are four basic types of question: closed, open, reflective and directive.

A closed question demands a defined answer, such as 'yes', 'no', '13 July', 'Nigel' or 'bricks'.

An open question demands further information from your prospects, for example, 'What do you think . . . ?', 'How do you see . . . ?'

The reflective question is one which reflects on answers already given, perhaps requesting further explanation of a particular point. Examples of this are 'You appear to be concerned . . .', 'Did I understand that . . . ?' Reflective questions give you the opportunity to make sure that you have understood the real meaning of what was said.

A directive question is usually asked to imply that there is a better way of doing things than the way they are being done now. Examples are: 'Explain to me exactly . . .', 'What happens when . . . ?'

Bottom line
Use questions to progressively develop your opportunities to sell. Your prospects will buy if, by your direction of the discussion, they begin to see for themselves the areas of concern within their companies.

*T*IP *8* Questioning Techniques

Asking plenty of open questions allows your prospects to talk about their business in general terms. They create a relaxed atmosphere, designed to start your prospects talking. By expanding your knowledge of your prospects, you can develop their needs and highlight opportunities. The needs that will be expressed are the requirements for change. For example, you may determine that current methods mean a stock check can be done in ten minutes. Your prospect's need may be to do it faster.

Open questions are used in the early stages of your Practical Selling Cycle and generally begin with: 'Who . . .?', 'What . . .?', 'When . . .?', 'Where . . .?', 'Why . . .?', and 'How . . .?'.

Reflective questions allow your prospects to reflect, think, consider or expand upon (or clarify) a statement or possible thought left unexpressed, so are useful in letting you home in on areas of opportunity. They may also be used to help determine if objections are real; to obtain opinions or concurrences; or to allow your prospects to respond (by offering them a choice of options). Reflective questions can take any form but usually *follow* some dialogue.

Directive questions are also useful, in that by using them to imply dissatisfaction, you imply that there is a better way – one which will involve your solution or service! Other uses of the directive question are:

● To determine sincerity of interest
● To reduce scope of interest or thought
● To control or re-direct the conversation or thinking
● To test the validity of thoughts or ideas expressed by your prospect
● To focus on an area of actual need
● To obtain positive agreement that the need is understood and necessary for business
● To obtain a direct answer.

Closed questions limit the amount of information you will receive from prospects. However, they can allow you to control the discussion by leading the prospect to a subject of your choice. For example 'May I tell you how my company's service will help to dramatically reduce that time?', or 'You were saying that you might have to increase staff to improve service. How many more would you need?'

Other types of questions you may come across include:

● *Restated questions:* these open with something like, 'Would you like me to expand upon . . .' While begging a yes or no answer, the chances are that you have obtained agreement to your initial points and the 'restatement' continues to push home the benefits of what you have to offer.
● *Justification questions:* 'What will it cost if you do not . . . ?'

- *Hypothetical questions:* 'What if . . . ?', 'Suppose . . . ?'
- *Exploratory questions:* 'Would you mind explaining . . . ?'
- *Leading questions:* 'How are you doing it now . . . ?'

Bottom line

Using effective questioning techniques to develop your prospect's needs will make it easier for you to successfully sell your solution. Use open questions to get information and opinions of a general nature; reflective ones to clarify and expand; directive ones to narrow your focus and verify areas of opportunity; and closed questions to confirm areas of agreement or concern.

To review the four basic types of question, open, reflective, directive, closed, identify the examples below:

1) How do you do the job now? _____
2) Why do you feel that you should make a change? _____
3) Would you elaborate on that? _____
4) Are you satisfied with your present results? _____
5) What do you intend to plan in your review? _____
6) Would there be anything keeping us from a favourable decision? _____
7) Then, Mr Jones, if I understand you correctly . . .? _____

8) Have you thought of the possibility of . . .? _____
9) That's very interesting . . . could you tell me more about it? _____
10) Who makes your buying decisions? _____
11) How often do you review your objectives? _____
*(Answers at foot of this page.)

Listen carefully to the answers to your questions. Don't start thinking about your next question or reply until you have heard and understood what has been said. Instead, learn to construct your next question from the previous response. Apart from forcing you to listen, this also helps you to keep the dialogue conversational.

Remember, always keep your questioning conversational. Try to comment on your prospect's answer prior to asking another question. Don't interrogate.

*ANSWERS: 1) open 2) directive 3) reflective 4) directive 5) open 6) directive 7) reflective 8) directive 9) reflective 10) closed 11) closed

STEP THREE

MAKE YOUR POSITION CLEAR

TIP 9 *Control the Conversation*

Friendly conversation and easy rapport between you and your prospects do little for sales unless you can guide and control the conversation, bringing it to an area of sales interest. To do this you need control techniques.

Once you know how to listen, question and maintain interest, you can apply several techniques to control the conversation – providing your prospects with an overview, establishing a frame of reference, taking the initiative and narrowing the focus to achieve your objectives.

Providing your prospects with an overview: it is important that prospects understand where you are going and can fill in the details as you proceed. Otherwise, you are asking them to understand each part of the puzzle as you give it to them, laying the burden on them to create the 'whole'.

Establishing a frame of reference: this means relating the benefits of your company, solution or service to your prospect's business, and using examples and comparisons with familiar things to help you make points quickly and effectively. This technique is particularly important when trying to communicate points which are abstract or unfamiliar to other people.

Taking the initiative: begin with the assumption that 75 per cent of what you are trying to communicate may not be received as you want it to be. Summarize, ask questions, clarify, seek opinions on your points and be sure to determine what action your prospect intends to take.

Bottom line
Keep narrowing the focus of the conversation until you achieve your objective, as follows:

- Uncover desires and problems and create needs
- Obtain agreement that the need exists
- Continually ask for feedback to ensure that you are understood.
- Develop the solution.

TIP *10* *Letters*

Letters are important in documenting your progress with prospects. If you intend to write, do it quickly: written communications should not destroy the momentum of your campaign.

Letters to prospects should be business-like and to the point, dealing only with important matters, not trivia or chat. To communicate effectively and efficiently in your letters, your text needs to be simple, straightforward and conversational in style.

Compare some of your letters with the following examples. A certain amount of licence has been taken with the 'bad' examples, although letters of a similar poor quality are not uncommon.

Letters

Mr R T Jones
Managing Director
G F Savings Ltd
15 Carthage Street
London SW1

Dear Mr Jones,

1 I simply wanted to tell you that I felt that our lunch was mutually beneficial. I discerned an inordinate amount of information and hope that you did as well.

2 These are arduous years for the business person. Life has grown excessively complex. Statistical configurations only serve to illuminate this simple fact. Because of this, it was edifying to read in this morning's paper that G F Savings plans a multiplicity of mini-branches to alleviate the problem.

3 Would it be feasible to give my company's role in this modularity concept some concrete consideration?

4 Perhaps we might meet again at a time that would be convenient to you.

Yours sincerely,

A. Pratt

1 *You discerned what?*

2 *This is called being 'in love with your own words'. If the fact, whatever it is, is simple, why are the words so complex?*

3 *What?!*

4 *When? What time? Probably never!*

Letters

```
Mr R T Jones
Managing Director
G F Savings Ltd
15 Carthage Street
London SW1

Dear Mr Jones,
```

1 A brief note to thank you for your time at our lunch meeting, which I very much enjoyed. I gained considerable insight into your problems and I hope that my information was useful to you.

2 In this morning's Telegraph, I noticed that G F Savings plan to open a number of mini-branches. It's an exciting concept and I believe that my company could be of assistance to you in this project.

3 I would like to discuss some proposals with you which I am confident will interest you. Would the afternoon of Tuesday, 16 June, be convenient? By then, I will have spoken with our own specialists and will have collected additional material pertinent to the subject.

Thank you for your time yesterday and I look forward to meeting you again.

Yours sincerely,

A. Star

1 *Straight, simple and conversational.*

2 *He's done his homework and gets right to the point.*

3 *He's suggesting a meeting (on a specific date and at a specific time) after additional information has been gathered. A credible approach.*

Letters

Ms P Rawlings
Managing Director
R T P Produce Ltd
The Chase
London W1

Dear Ms Rawlings,

1   Pursuant to our telephone conversation on Thursday, 28 March,
I would like to take this opportunity to suggest that we meet at
your convenience.

2   At that aforementioned time, we could discuss, in depth, the
current state of your present installation and the possible
improvements that might be made.

3   Therefore, I shall call you in several days to see if we can set
up an appointment.

4   I look forward to our meeting.

Yours sincerely,

A. Pratt

1   *This is pure
lawyer-talk.*

2   *No specific date suggested.*

3   *Why write the letter
at all? Nothing suggested.
No action was called for.*

4   *He'll be disappointed!*

Letters

Ms P Rawlings
Managing Director
R T P Produce Ltd
The Chase
London W1

Dear Ms Rawlings,

1 I enjoyed meeting you on Thursday and would like to take this
   opportunity to suggest that we meet again next Friday, 12 June, at
   3 p.m.

2 I realize that you're concerned with your present installation
   and, at that time, we could discuss in-depth improvements
   that would prove extremely valuable to your company.

3 I look forward to our meeting.

Yours sincerely,

A. Star

1 *No beating about the bush.*

2 *Advantages and benefits.*

3 *. . . and it's a meeting
   he'll get.*

STEP FOUR

COUNTER THOSE OBJECTIONS

EMPATHY

'I certainly understand how you feel,
many of my customers have felt as you do,
but they have found that . . .'

FEEL
↓
FELT
↓
FOUND

TIP *11* *The Objection*

Even though most of us think of objections as something negative, they do form a vital part in the progress of the big deal. They open up lines of communication by making you aware of how your prospects are thinking when they object to your suggestions and proposals, and this awareness can help you.

Objections can work to your advantage if they indicate that your prospect is:

● Paying attention to your proposals
● Interested enough to consider possibilities
● Seeking further information
● Evaluating your proposal.

Objections can warn you that you need to change your tactics if they indicate that your prospect is:

● Stalling
● Concealing something
● Making excuses
● Not interested.

If the prospect is genuinely interested in your proposals and seeking information, you are then in a position to increase that interest by providing that information. If the prospect is stalling, concealing or making excuses, you must chip away at the objections until the prospect faces the need to take action.

Bottom line
Objections are statements that enable you to progress further. Listen to their meaning and act accordingly.

OBJECTION

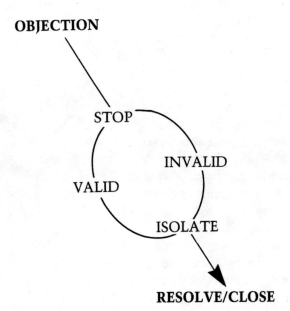

STOP

INVALID

VALID

ISOLATE

RESOLVE/CLOSE

TIP 12 *Capitalize on the Opportunity*

When handling an objection, think carefully about the *reason* behind the objection. Listen, question, identify: is the objection genuine or false?

A genuine objection is one that is recognized as a reasonable obstacle to the sale. It can be a positive buying signal.

A false objection is one that is recognized as disguising a genuine objection, an excuse or an attempt to avoid involvement in a selling situation.

Both genuine and false objections can block a sale, so you must learn to listen to and manage them. Don't let objections overpower you to the extent that you begin to doubt that the sale can be made. It is your role to sell to your prospects; don't let them sell to you.

Remember, your challenge is to convince your prospects of your viewpoint and not to let them convince you of theirs. Test each objection until your prospect either agrees with you and has no reason not to buy, or is forced into revealing another objection, perhaps the real one, which you can then test.

Bottom line
If you are unwilling to test your prospect's objections, or are too willing to accept them, then you are giving up without a fight – not the mark of a successful salesperson.

Remember

IF YOU HAVE NO OBJECTIONS, YOU HAVE
NO PROSPECT
↓
EVERY OBJECTION IS AN OPPORTUNITY
TO CLOSE
↓

TIP 13 — Objections are a Natural Process

Objections can occur at all phases of the sales cycle:

- **During the first phase:** for example, a secretary may block you, or prospects may claim to be busy. This may be because they are prejudiced against salespeople or wish to test you.
- **Whilst you develop the need:** your prospects may conceal their feelings from you. They may stall, or make excuses, or simply refuse to listen.
- **Whilst recognizing needs:** your prospects may not reveal all the facts to you. Perhaps they resent giving information to an outsider.
- **Whilst you engineer prospect awareness:** prospects may not agree with the analyis of their problems or needs when related to their company's goals and objectives. They may not agree with your criteria, or accept you as being qualified to assess their needs.
- **As you present solutions:** prospects may not agree that results will be produced as you have presented them.
- **Whilst you try to close the order:** prospects may have second thoughts about the need for results or the desirability for change, or the value of your solution or service compared with others.

Since many opinions may be involved in a prospect's purchase decision, especially for that bigger deal, you should be prepared for objections at every level of management. Top management may agree with you but functional management may raise all kinds of objections, or *vice versa*. Middle management may like your company, solutions and services while top management think otherwise. Your primary contact may raise objections while other levels of management favour your proposals.

Bottom line
It is unlikely that all the people involved in a big deal will want to go ahead. So, expect objections, and take care that they are:

CALMLY NOTED
↓
CONSIDERED RESPECTFULLY
↓
COUNTERED SKILFULLY

TIP 14 *Spot the Objection*

Recognize objections

It's one thing to say you should expect objections, but how do you recognize them when they arise?

First, a word of caution. When your prospect asks a question, usually he or she is simply requesting information. A salesperson may nervously mistake a question for an objection. However, a question, if left unanswered – or if answered incorrectly – could develop into an objection. For example:

'How much is it?'

'There is a wide price range from . . . to . . . but at this stage I'm not sure which would be the best for your company.'

If price is an objection, prospects will make it clear after that answer. If not, they will accept that form of answer.

When your prospect raises an objection, you must manage it. Salespeople are sometimes so preoccupied with their own objectives, they forget to listen and think. As a result, they mismanage objections. Managing objections involves all your skills of communication. But, above all, you must practise.

Bottom line

Be sure a prospect's interest is an objection before reacting. If, in the example above, your prospect says, 'Even your lowest price is too much', then you have an objection.

TIP 15
Qualify the Genuine Objection

There are a few steps which will help you to bring your skills to bear on an objection.

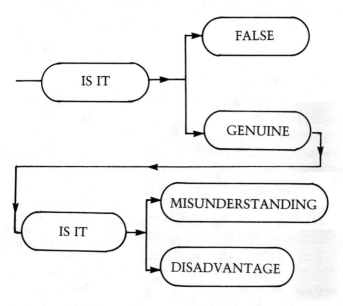

Determine whether the objection is genuine or false.

Genuine objections are easy to recognize because they concern a misunderstanding or a disadvantage.

If the objection results from a misunderstanding, you must clarify precisely what your prospect understands and then clear up any misunderstanding by a restatement of the facts. Genuine objections, resulting from a misunderstanding, are not uncommon. They usually result from poor communication between the salesperson and the prospect or misinterpretation. For instance, your prospect may not have understood all that is included in the price you have given, and an explanation may satisfy these concerns.

Objections concerning a disadvantage can be slightly more tricky. For example, your prospect may have seen a similar solution at a lower price, making your offer less attractive. You must now sell the advantages of your company, solution and your service to outweigh the disadvantages that exist in your prospect's mind. You can do this by strongly presenting the benefits of dealing with your company to minimize the significance of any feature (often unimportant) that your solution or service may not possess. Continuing the price example, these benefits must be seen to overcome the price difference. You will invariably win if your company has the stronger customer-care policy.

Bottom line
Always qualify an objection. Misunderstood? Explain. Disadvantaged? Sell your benefits to outweigh any difference.

False objections are all objections which are not concerned with misunderstandings or disadvantages. They are excuses which your prospect might use for not wanting to buy.

False objections are very common
Prospects give excuses for many reasons. They may want something else which, for the moment, is more important. For example, solutions to problems with which they are currently preoccupied. On the other hand, they may be afraid to admit needs exist, out of fear of the unknown, or fear of responsibility for change, or fear of possible failure (especially where significant expenditure is involved), or simply out of fear of losing control.

Don't give up
Your challenge as a salesperson is to divert your prospect's attention from immediate preoccupations to the needs that you would like to develop and stress. You do this by backing away from the excuses given and re-approaching your prospect in terms of those needs. You must then get agreement from your prospect as to the importance of those needs, which you can then satisfy. Try asking the question, 'If you had implemented my company's proposal in the past and you were now obtaining the benefits I have just described, would they be helping your business today?' If you have sold your benefits well and objections are really only excuses not

to order now, the answer can only be 'yes'. This will be because your prospect is being asked to consider benefits and not concerns.

Bottom line
False objections are excuses. Divert prospects' attention from these excuses by re-approaching and developing their needs.

TIP 17

The Do's and Don'ts of Handling Objections

React positively – never be defensive or indignant.

● An objection is a challenge and calls upon you to use your communication skills.
● Each time you overcome one, you will gain confidence in your ability to manage the wide variety of objections that will be presented to you during your sales calls.

Respect your prospects' opinions. Because it is vital to keep the lines of communication open, never *ever* get into an argument with a prospect. Don't put prospects down – allow them to save face if they are mistaken. Respecting a prospect's opinion builds his or her image of you, and that of the company you represent.

Be enthusiastic about your company, solution or service. Always stress how it meets identified needs and show how the needs that are met compensate for any deficiencies your prospect might observe.

Be professional.

● Always speak the truth.
● Never guess, exaggerate or misrepresent, and *never* fabricate answers.
● If you don't know the answer to a question, or aren't sure, admit it. Tell your prospect that you'll find out the answer, and be sure to do so.

Be well-organized. Make a note of objections raised. Not only does this demonstrate that you take them seriously, but also helps you build up a list of the most common to help you in future sales calls.

The bottom line
When handling objections, try to work to the cycle illustrated on page 57.

Grow with experience. Expect objections and don't regard them as unpleasant chores.

● Every objection that you recognize and successfully manage is a major step towards the close.
● Every objection that you successfully manage gives you an insight into your prospect's expectations and needs.
● Every objection that you successfully manage will increase your self-confidence.

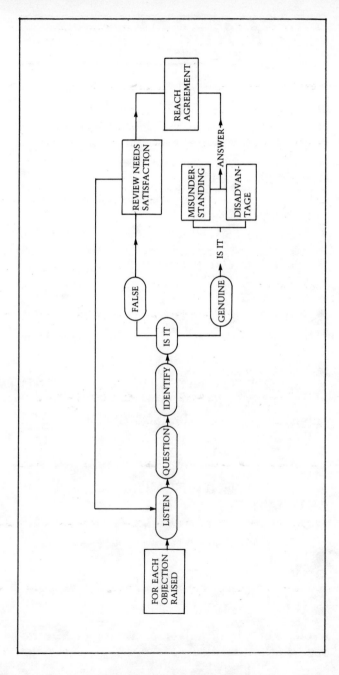

FOR EACH OBJECTION RAISED → LISTEN → QUESTION → IDENTIFY → IS IT

IS IT → FALSE → REVIEW NEEDS SATISFACTION

IS IT → GENUINE → IS IT

IS IT → MISUNDERSTANDING → ANSWER
IS IT → DISADVANTAGE → ANSWER

REVIEW NEEDS SATISFACTION → REACH AGREEMENT

TIP 18 *Golden Rules*

- KEEP CALM
- LISTEN AND UNDERSTAND
- BE ALERT
- ANTICIPATE
- SHOW INTEREST
- IDENTIFY AND ISOLATE THE OBJECTION
- RESOLVE THE OBJECTION
- DRAW OUT THE OBJECTION
- STICK TO THE POINT
- AVOID IRRELEVANCES
- NET IT OUT
- KEEP IT IN PERSPECTIVE
- NEVER TELL PROSPECTS THAT THEY'RE WRONG
- BE OBSERVANT
- REASON FOR NOT BUYING MAY END UP REASON TO BUY
- NEVER LET PERSONALITIES GET INVOLVED
- HEAR YOUR PROSPECTS OUT
- NEVER ARGUE
- TRY TO FIND HUMOROUS SIDE OF SITUATION
- DON'T GET TRAPPED BY OBJECTIONS THAT WILL GO AWAY
- AVOID 'I'
- AVOID 'YES, BUT . . .'
- DON'T GUESS
- AFTER HANDLING, TRIAL CLOSE

Remember, objections are simply one more opportunity to sell!

STEP FIVE

PLAN THAT SALES CALL

TIP *19*   *The Need to Plan*

Successful selling is not guaranteed by hard work. You must also make effective use of your time by planning who to call on, and when to call on them, and by developing a specific plan for each call in order to achieve your objectives.

Planning will build your prospect's trust and confidence in you as an organized individual. It will help you to minimize failures and maximize success. Finally, it will enable you to prioritize your own activities and tell you where you stand relative to your goals.

When you see your prospects, you must have clear objectives and a strategy that you wish to follow. You should have an objective for each call: unplanned calls are usually a waste of time, except when canvassing prospects. Before calling you should have reviewed your prospect's background, reviewed previous call reports on the account, and re-evaluated what it will take to close the order.

Bottom line
Having a strategy forces logical thinking as a basis for making decisions. It reminds you of what steps still need to be taken to close the order.

Having a strategy enables you to evaluate your performance and improve your tactics.

T_{IP} 20 *Do You Know Where You're Going?*

For large accounts, you may have to make several sales calls to reach your objective. In the case of a major account, the order may be closed many months after the first call. The purpose of each individual call may vary, but will be related to the overall objectives.

Always plan a primary and secondary objective for each sales call. Pursue the primary objective, realizing that your prospect's responses may force you to improvise: your ability to think quickly here is paramount.

As the interview progresses, you may have to refine, expand and revise your plan. Put yourself in your prospect's shoes, and set an alternative plan before you make your call.

Bottom line

If you don't know where you're going, you'll never get there. In addition to setting objectives, it's also good practice to ask yourself three questions:

1) What are the benefits that will accrue to my prospect as a result of seeing me?
2) Why would he or she want to accept my proposals?
3) What else could I be doing to help my prospect to a positive decision?

STEP SIX

BIG DEALS ARE LOGICAL

$T_{IP}21$ *The Practical Selling Cycle*

The Practical Selling Cycle consists of one, or many, sales calls. Normally, the number of sales calls required to successfully complete the cycle is dependent upon the size and complexity of the order in relation to your effectiveness. Each of the calls you make will have three identifiable parts: the opening, the body and the close.

The opening of a sales call is usually quite brief and requires the following skills:

- **Gaining attention:** Successfully opening the sales call is an important milestone towards achieving the purpose of your call. You must gain the attention of your prospects quickly – to you and to your subject. The first thirty seconds are critical.
- **Knowing what to say:** Develop a professional introduction and keep perfecting it. Develop industry knowledge so that you can relate specifically to your prospect's business. Be careful of tricky openings employing gimmicks – they can fail miserably. You must *earn* the right to your prospect's time.
- **Establishing rapport:**
  - On any call, genuine discussion of a subject of personal interest to your prospect can break the ice in a professional manner. A sincere compliment regarding a topic of obvious interest to the other person will also help.
  - If this is the first call, an introduction or

reference from another person may help.

- If it is a follow-up call, you should summarize the conclusions of the previous call, securing agreement from your prospect that your summary is correct.
- Always give your prospect a concise statement of your purpose in calling.

The body of the call is its substance. It's here that you begin to accomplish what you came for, making progress within the Practical Selling Cycle. Specific techniques employed in the body of a sales call will vary, but will almost invariably include:

- *Questioning:* gather facts and expand the points related to your stated purpose. You must secure your prospect's participation. The greater his or her participation, the greater your mutual understanding. Plan questions that will determine your prospect's reactions to your ideas. The best way to secure participation is through questions that cannot be answered with 'yes' or 'no'.
- *Listening:* appreciate your prospect's points of view. Look for key thoughts in what they say; watch their gestures; evaluate what they are telling you. Do not concentrate on what you are going to say next.
- *Presenting your ideas:* throughout the body of the call, you will not only be identifying your prospect's needs, but also gaining agree-

ment that they truly exist. You will also, therefore, be presenting solutions and alternatives. In stressing your ideas, be sure to focus on *benefits to the prospect* rather than on features or methods of use.

● *Summarizing:* always summarize your understanding of what has been discussed and agreed.

After the body of the call, it is time to end or close the sales call. As well as summarizing what you and your prospects have discussed and agreed, you will have answered any questions or objections that have been raised. In the larger account environment, and assuming that this is one of many calls, you will establish the next step and secure commitment for future action. This will often include an introduction to others involved in the decision-making process.

Bottom line
Don't try and move too quickly. Keep checking back to ensure that you haven't missed anything and that you have a clear understanding of the total picture as presented by your prospect.

TIP22 *Think Logically*

The Practical Selling Cycle focuses on your prospect by determining buying motives and needs, by making your prospect aware of those needs and then closing the order. Knowledge of the stages ensures that you know exactly where you are in the overall process and provides you with a competitive advantage. As you become more familiar with it, you will realize that it is based on logic, and this realization will help you to remember the steps in the cycle.

Your prospect is a busy person. To take up an amount of their time, you must earn the right to that time, through the gaining of their attention and interest. In a word, though *rapport*. You must stimulate your prospect to think about a different way to run his or her business. Creating a productive environment in which you both feel that you can work with each other will lead to your prospect's co-operation as you proceed through the sale.

In order to be convinced of his or her need for your solution, your prospect must first be *aware* of that need.

A WINNER MAKES COMMITMENTS

A LOSER MAKES PROMISES

In brief:

Recognition of needs
Through effective questioning, listening and evaluation of your prospects' responses, you confirm – in your own mind – your prospects' real needs, as developed in 'need development'.

Prospect awareness and agreement to needs
Through effective questioning, listening and the use of sales aids, where appropriate. The gaining of your prospects' agreement to the identified needs and that they will implement your solution, provided that it is considered viable. To understand who will make the final decision and on what basis.

Presentation of your solution
Now that your prospect is aware of the problems that exist, a solution can be presented to deal with them. Here you will be gaining support and commitment to your proposed solution at all levels within your prospect's organization, including the appropriate and responsible financial officer. You will be confirming that your proposal is the correct business decision.

The close
The most important and exciting of steps – the close – follows naturally and logically if all the preceding steps have been managed well.

Bottom line
Effective calls, presentations and proposals that

you make within the logical sequence of the Practical Selling Cycle, together with sound objectives and action plans, will ensure success.

TIP 23
Earning the Right – an Ongoing Process

The need to earn the right is an on-going one, especially in a long sales cycle, where attention and interest must be generated across many different levels. Never forget that you are often an interruption, even when an appointment has been made. Your prospect has many important tasks and activities to attend to, so, logically, it is up to you to ensure that he or she is attending to you and not simply giving the appearance of attending.

● Introduce yourself and your company
● Thank your prospects for their time
● Convey warmth and interest. This can be communicated by a firm handshake, a pleasant smile and an open, intelligent expression
● Appear confident, enthusiastic and respectful
● Appearance goes a long way to creating that positive image and the image that you would want to project is typified by the well-groomed, tailored appearance
● Be prepared for the interview. There is nothing so unnerving as the feeling of being afloat, without direction. Not only does this uncertainty give you uncomfortable moments, but it is also wasteful of your precious sales time. Don't get into the habit of trying to 'wing it'. Have an objective for every call. Have specific questions for which you require answers
● Use those open questions to get your prospects talking
● Know your prospect's business. That doesn't

mean that you have to be an expert on every industry, but good listening, along with the posing of one or two intelligent questions, is one of the best ways of improving your knowledge of your prospect's business

● As you initially engage your prospects in conversation, try to assess their individual traits. Are they enthusiastic, direct, indecisive, withdrawn or uninterested? Adapt your approach depending on type.

At the start of a sales campaign, you may have to call across many different departments and talk to many people before you find interest. In addition, top and middle management, financial and operations management all have different interests. Even within the same department, different interests may exist: usually, top management are interested in overall profitability, while middle management are concerned with the implementation of plans to ensure the achievement of their company goals.

You cannot, therefore, secure and maintain genuine interest by talking in general terms. You must develop interest at all levels. You must *earn the right* at all levels.

Bottom line
Prospects buy from people they like. Earning the right effectively, through gaining attention, developing that interest and establishing rapport gives you the start – and the momentum – that you need to successfully close those sales.

TIP24

Need Development –
Logically

Listening and continued questioning broadens
the scope of interest. This questioning is a two-
way conversation – not an interrogation! It
involves listening closely to what your prospects are saying. Their contribution will, in
part, guide your questions. Alternatively, it will
suggest questions which allow your prospects
to:

- Provide information on a point (open questions)
- Elaborate and/or clarify a point (reflective
  questions)
- Answer yes or no as you narrow the focus
  (directive questions)

At all times, you will be relating your
prospects needs to the overall aims and objectives of their companies. If you cannot develop
a need, you have no basis on which to continue
the Practical Selling Cycle. Remember, there is
no end to developing needs, and the more
knowledge that you have of your prospects, the
stronger your position to eventually close that
sale.

More often than not, your prospects will not
have evaluated their companys' real needs, and
this presents you with an oppportunity to:

- Fully examine their needs and ensure that
  these are perceived correctly

● Determine whether it is greater, or less, than your prospects recognize
● Decide how well your solution is appropriate to their key needs
● Clarify or expand these areas of interest by use of reflective questions
● Broaden that knowledge of your prospect's business and thereby improve your chances to clearly highlight their needs.

Bottom line
Question and *listen*. Question and *listen*. Question and *listen*.

A WINNER LISTENS

A LOSER JUST WAITS UNTIL IT'S HIS OR HER TURN TO TALK

TIP 25

Recognizing Needs – Logically

Once you have focused on areas of interest and have developed needs related to your prospect's overall aims and objectives, you are ready to test those needs.

You will be considering all aspects of your solution and service knowledge as you listen to your prospects. As areas of need are identified, you will begin to recognize the solution or service which will satisfy that need most effectively. But, although an area of interest exists, you cannot assume that a need exists. You must determine if there is a need in their area of interest, in their industry – or if there is a need in one area and interest in another.

To confirm that need, you must know the answers to the following questions, and you should structure your questions to elicit these responses:

- Why does my prospect want this, or that, result?
- Is the result really needed?
- How are results currently obtained?
- Will the results profit my prospect's business?

Bottom line
Even though the need may be obvious to you as you listen to the conversation, it may not necessarily be obvious to your prospect.

Unless you have agreement from your solution that a need exists, you cannot present a solution. Your objective at this point is to establish that your prospect is dissatisfied with the present methods of running his or her business. You do this by:

● Asking reflective questions to induce this dissatisfaction. This forces your prospect to reflect and admit needs

● Replaying needs in problem form, to increase dissatisfaction. 'Do you feel that the delays in getting at your stock may affect your level of customer satisfaction?'

● Reviewing results that could be obtained and creating needs for those results. For example, 'the implementation of our service does not require more people and will speed this process. This will ensure an excellent return on investment for your company as increased customer satisfaction brings more business'

● Creating a sense of urgency for these results, so enhancing the probability of closing the sale. For example, 'our solution has proved so easy to use that you will find your staff much more interested in completing their tasks as they feel, and are, more productive'

● Using sales aids (supportive visuals), which help you focus your prospect's attention on the value of satisfaction and therefore on the opportunities that are being missed at present. This may generate the dissatisfaction with their present methods that you desire.

A WINNER SAYS, 'LET'S FIND OUT'

A LOSER SAYS, 'NOBODY KNOWS'

Bottom line
Ask yourself again the following questions to confirm the needs and truly qualify your prospect:

● Why does my prospect want this, or that, result?
● Is the result really needed?
● How are results currently obtained?
● Will the results profit my prospect's business?

Questions to consider while establishing need and qualifying are:

	YES	NO
● Are your prospects prepared and able to buy?	☐	☐
● Are you calling at the right level?	☐	☐

- Who are the decision-makers?
- Who are the recommenders?
- Who are the influencers?
- Who is involved in the approval cycle?
- Who is involved in the procurement cycle?

● Do you have an 'inside' salesperson and who is he or she?	☐	☐
● Is need recognized, and agreed to, by the decision-makers and recommenders?	☐	☐
● Is executive management aware of the need and do they concur with the need?	☐	☐
● Have the various levels of management agreed to favourably consider the solution?	☐	☐
● Are the prospects prepared to commit their resources (time, people, money) in implementing your proposal?	☐	☐
● Are your prospects willing to change their way of doing busi-	☐	☐

ness to implement your solution?

● Did you manage to avoid getting locked into one management level? □ □

● If you were blocked at a certain level, did you find a way out? □ □

● Did you call high and broad in your accounts to define the need, qualify your prospects and sell your solution? □ □

TIP 27

Presenting Your Solution – Logically

The purpose of presenting your plan or solution is to gain formal agreement that it satisfies needs that have previously been agreed and valued against measurable criteria. You will contrast the present method with your proposal, stressing the advantages and gaining your prospect's reactions.

The format of the presentation isn't as important as the content:

- Does your proposal satisfy the need(s)?
- Does your proposal meet the requirement(s)?
- Does your proposal increase the sense of urgency?
- Does your proposal cause action?

You will be confirming to your prospects that your proposal is the best possible business decision.

Depending on the complexity of your solution or service, you may need to make one or more presentations. If the communication of different benefits is necessary then your different presentations should reflect this. An early presentation should:

- Paint a general picture of your solution
- Emphasize the particular interests of the individual being addressed
- Show that the solution meets your prospect's needs and requirements and describe the associated results and benefits

● Obtain a 'yes' answer to the question, 'Can I count on your unqualified support during my final presentation?'. If your prospect still seems to be stalling, find out why and overcome the objection(s) before your presentation, until you get that 'yes' answer – this 'yes' will minimize the likelihood of someone jumping up during the final presentation with a 'But . . .'.

The final presentation is the high spot of your selling efforts. In it you should:

● Thank individuals for their past co-operation and time (where previous presentations have been made at various levels within the company)
● Review your plan and solution
● Obtain formal agreement from the decision-maker that your plan or solution satisfies identified and agreed needs that have been defined earlier in the selling process
● Carefully handle any questions so that the presentation is not side-tracked to a discussion of topics unrelated to the purpose of the presentation. If preliminary presentations have been made, tactfully refer the question back to these
● Ask for the order.

Bottom line
Your final presentation is always given to those

people in your accounts who individually, or collectively, are empowered to make that final decision. You must practise and rehearse this presentation – and ask for the order!

TIP *28*   *The Logical Close*

The close is that definitive request for that final commitment. It's why you are a salesperson. It's moving your prospect over a psychological barrier – to the point of no more resistance; to the point of committing him or her to a firm order.

Many 'salespeople' are afraid of asking for the order. But if the Practical Selling Cycle has been followed, asking for the order should not be a surprise to anyone. In fact, your decision-makers expect you to ask them. They would be disappointed if you didn't! It is the only logical conclusion to your sales campaign, and there are several logical techniques for proceeding to it, and handling it successfully.

The 'trial' close is a useful technique. Though not necessarily an attempt to close the sale, it attempts to determine readiness to buy. Its purpose is to seek agreement on key points being discussed, with the responses giving you an indication as to how close your prospect is to a decision.

There are several techniques you can use in trial closes, each of which is designed to seek agreement, obtain an opinion or gain a reaction. You can:

● *Ask a direct question*: 'Will you approve the order today?' or 'Do you agree that the benefits we've discussed will be of value to you?'
● *Ask a 'choice' question*: 'Do you feel that

a . . . would be adequate or would you like to consider . . .?'

● *Make a factual statement to seek an opinion*: 'Your present method needs . . . which only our . . . can provide.'

● *Make a provocative statement to gain a reaction*: 'The . . . of my company's proposal will not only improve that department's productivity but will also immediately improve . . .'.

The purpose of each question is to obtain an answer, reaction, opinion or other statement which you can then evaluate to determine your prospect's readiness to buy. In addition, these techniques will also draw out objections, which can then be resolved before your final close. Like everything else in good salespersonship, becoming adept at trial closing takes practice.

To be successful at closing, you need to be familiar with various personality types. People are different from one another – in their desires, values, motives and needs. They may also differ widely in their responses to you. To sell to them, you must address these differences. If you understand them, you can improve your communications and enhance your sales success. From a sales point of view, there are four basic personality types:

● Intuitor (expressive) Original, creative, idealistic

● Thinker (analytical) — Deliberate, objective, logical, rational

● Feeler (feeler) — People-orientated, loyal, warm

● Sensor (driver) — Action-orientated, multi-functional, impatient.

Intuitors tend to over-generalize in their statements, think of the future and get excited by long-range trends. They understand very clearly how their function or department fits into the big picture, and place a high value on new ideas, concepts and theories. They are imaginative, creative and charismatic, preferring to avoid detail in favour of examining the widest range of opportunities. Their enthusiasm means they may often appear impatient with others who do not see the value of their ideas.

Thinkers tend to offer *more* detail than necessary (ask them the time, and they'll build a clock). They place a high value on logic, observation and rational principles. At worst, they can be indecisive and overly analytical. They are also good communicators, and take a comprehensive view of the past, present and future when making decisions.

Feelers are dynamic, loyal, impulsive and people-orientated. They are good at listening and at predicting the behaviour of others. Because they make decisions at 'gut level', they are often poor at analyzing detail.

Sensors are impatient, direct and often ruthless in achieving their goals. They thrive on getting things done, usually by themselves as they are extremely reluctant delegators. Their love of speed and dislike of detail means they are quick decision-makers.

By taking time to understand these characteristics of your decision-makers, recommenders and influencers, you will put yourself in a better position to have your proposals accepted.

There are many other techniques which can be applied to closing, some of them simply extensions of the trial close techniques referred to earlier.

The *ask-them-to-buy technique* is best used when you have encountered little or no resistance. This assumes that all objections have been overcome and handled successfully. The secure and confident decision-maker is likely to appreciate straightforwardness. But always be aware that such directness may scare the insecure individual and cause resistance. Questions might include, 'Are we ready to proceed?', 'What do I need to do for you to approve this order?', 'Are we in agreement?'

Some salespeople find it difficult to use this technique because of that common disinclination to 'rock the boat'. But, if under the above circumstances, you cannot ask for the order, then you will never be a successful salesperson. The selling process cannot continue for ever and this technique brings it to a head.

Remember, if you use this technique, ask for the order directly, then keep quiet. Once you've asked for the order, the person who speaks first loses!

In many cases, merely assuming that you are going to get the order can actually lead to the order itself. It involves the power of suggestion and must be done carefully so as to avoid looking weak and transparent. Effective assumptive closers maintain a very positive frame-of-mind regarding their ability to close the order. They assume that the order is assured and, if your prospect has confidence in you, this technique will be successful. If there has been that friendly and courteous (but effective) seller/buyer relationship, then your prospect is more likely to accept your assumption as fact.

As with the trial close, the assumptive technique is certain to bring out any latent sales resistance or objections. By assuming that you have the order, you force your prospects to raise objections quickly.

The *'choice' technique* is also an assumptive technique, providing leverage by leading your prospect to reveal a preference. Two choices are given but either answer is a commitment, for example, 'Would you like to . . . in March or June?' The assumption is made that your prospect is ready to buy. The answer tells you whether to go for the order, or whether the assumption was incorrect, in which case additional work will be needed before the close can be made.

A *summary* of all the points of agreement can often induce that positive buying decision. This technique is one of the most helpful, providing the easiest transition from presentation to close.

If the closing does not occur at your final presentation and has to be postponed to some later date, you must bridge the gap in time between presentation and close. To do this, briefly summarize the need, major requirements and key benefits of your proposed solution. Seek agreement to this summary and then ask for the commitment to buy.

You might use the *'subordinate decision' technique*. This is where you get your prospect to decide upon something of a subordinate or secondary importance, for example, 'Who will be the user of . . .?' assumes that your prospect wants your solution or service in the first place. This is a common technique in the selling of large, expensive items because it eases a decision involving a large monetary outlay. It is an invaluable technique when you have noted a favourable reaction to one or more aspects of your proposal during your presentations.

The *'impending event' technique* is a form of closing based upon the use of some outside, or future, event that should prompt a decision. Your prospects are advised to take action now, placing the order early and saving their company money, for example, 'We need to schedule . . . to ensure that delivery takes place prior to your peak season'. Generally, this technique should only be used when more conventional closing methods have failed. It is, however, particularly appropriate when a complacent prospect persists in delaying the decision for no substantive reason. It must be accomplished with great tact to avoid giving the appearance of a high-pressure salesperson.

The *'question' technique* can be employed when your prospect raises a concealed objection, such as, 'I want to think it over'. A series of questions and statements must be chained together. For example, you could review your benefits, making sure that your prospects agree with each one. Then ask specifically what their concerns are. This will get their objections into the open, so that you can repeat and re-phrase them to verify understanding. Once the objection is identified, answer it in the terminology opposite to that of the objection, for example, 'It's too complex'. Answer: 'It's really quite simple . . .' Always get your prospect's agreement that each objection has been successfully handled.

The *'be a leader' technique* plays on the advantages of being first, on notions of innovation and pioneering. Your proposal is described to your prospect as a way to continue to be a leader in his or her field. This can only be used with those prospects you know well and who you know enjoy being leaders. Other prospects might well perceive such challenges as threats.

The Logical Close

The *'cost versus value' technique* ('you can't afford not to . . .') is used to compare benefits with cost and is helpful in showing your prospect the value of your proposal by showing a good return on the proposed investment. Naturally, you must have collected the data you need while building your sale. If your prospect has provided this financial input, owing to your skilful questioning during that building, it will be his/her facts that support your proposal, and any objections raised will be difficult for your prospect to sustain.

The *'conditional' technique* involves some form of perceived exchange. You agree to fulfil a particular obligation in return for the order. Trial closes, using this technique, can be used throughout your sales campaign, for example, 'If I can . . . can I take it that you will . . .'

As a final close, the question becomes, 'You agree that, if I could . . . you would . . . As we have agreed that . . ., will you now approve the order?'

The *'suppositional' technique* is similar to the conditional close, but simpler. It is used as a way out when your prospect is in a state of indecision over a minor objection. For example, 'If it were . . ., would you place the order?'

The *'provisional order' technique* should not be used unless unavoidable. In bigger deals, it may be, for example, that Board approval is required. It is often difficult for a decision-maker to say 'no' to your proposal after lengthy negotiation and agreement has taken place, even though Board approval is required. Your prospect, therefore, may approve your proposal without any responsibility, but is committed to confirm the Board's approval at a later date.

A simple but useful closing method is the *'reference' technique*. This simply means referring to a customer of your company who is well-known and respected.

It is not important that you are able to name closing techniques. What is important is that you are able to use them effectively. You must establish your own library of trial closes and closing techniques. You will find that, within your personal style, certain techniques will be more effective than others. By identifying those that work well, you will eventually reach the point where you use those techniques readily and with ease.

It is time to simply ask for the order and then shut up when:

● You and your prospect are in line with each other
● Your prospect has enough information to make a decision
● Your prospect's attitudes are positive (excited)
● You see positive body language (smiles, relaxation, friendliness)
● You hear positive remarks ('I like that')
● Your prospect appears confident

- Your prospect likes your proposal
- Your prospect realizes he or she can afford it
- Your prospect realizes he or she can't afford to be without it
- Your prospect realizes the benefits

If, having tried all the appropriate techniques in your repertoire, you still fail to close, use the *'doorknob' technique*:

- Smile.
- Thank your prospect for his/her time, leaving the door open for future sales. Your prospect will relax.
- Then ask them what you did wrong, what you didn't do, why you didn't get a favourable decision.
- Pause for an answer – the real objection may surface.
- Go for the close again!

Bottom line
Ask for the order and SHUT UP!

STEP SEVEN

THE CHECKLIST

The Checklist

1) Earn the right
   - develop rapport
   - gain attention
   - appear confident
   - assess your prospect
   - suit approach to individual
   - show genuine interest
2) Need development
   - ask general and specific questions
   - listen
   - analyze
3) Recognition of needs
   - ask specific questions
   - confirm real needs
   - match your solution or service
4) Prospect awareness and agreement of needs
   - restate needs in problem form
   - create a sense of urgency
5) Present solution
   - present logical solution
   - confirm sound business decision
   - gain agreement that needs will be satisfied
6) The close
   - smooth transition from presentation
   - ask for the order and be quiet!

APPROACH CALL EVALUATION (EXAMPLE)

Account: A. N. OTHER   **Contact:** NIGEL HENZELL-THOMAS

Call objective: IDENTIFY REQUIREMENTS / NEEDS. AGREE WITH CLIENT. DETERMINE NEXT STEP WITH CLIENT

QUESTIONS/KEY RESPONSES

EARN THE RIGHT PURPOSE, ROLE, TIME FRAME.

NEED DEVELOPMENT WHAT KIND OF COMPANY? YOUR POSITION, RESPONSIBILITIES, COMPANY GOALS.

SALES AWARENESS OBJECTIVES/GOALS DISCUSSED RELATIVE TO OFFERINGS.

CUSTOMER AWARENESS DID NOT LEAD CUSTOMER TOO SOON.

	COMMENTS
Questioning Skills (need development)	
● Used appropriate questions. Probed until all/most relevant needs discovered .... ☐	ASKED ABOUT QUALITY REQUIREMENTS AND TIME FRAMES.
● Questioning techniques occasionally effective. Some needs revealed .... ☑	'DEVELOPED' RELATIONSHIP. DID
● Used few appropriate questions. Did little probing of customer responses. Only a few needs discovered .... ☐	NOT ESTABLISH DELEGATABLE TASKS.

Questioning Skills (customer awareness)

● Consistent use of effective open, reflective and directive questions to create prospect understanding/acknowledgement of needs . . . .   ☐

● Occasionally used effective open, reflective and directive questions to create understanding . . . .   ☑   USED FEW DIRECTIVE QUESTIONS TO UPSET PROSPECT'S EQUILIBRIUM.

● Used few open, reflective and directive questions to create understanding . . . .   ☐

Listening Skills

● Recognized/analyzed feedback. Developed presentation based on information received . . . .   ☐   O.K. ON QUALITY AND TURNAROUND. DID NOT PURSUE OR PICK UP ON DELEGATION.

● Recognized feedback. Made frequent, but not always successful, attempts to build upon the information received . . . .   ☑

● Customer input seldom registered. Asked redundant questions. Failed to develop the information given . . . .   ☐

Objections

- Properly questioned, tested and overcame objections ☐
- Did not always properly question/test objections before overcoming them ☐
- Questioned/tested objections, but seldom overcame effectively ☑   TRIED TO OVERCOME OBJECTION BEFORE ISOLATING.
- Seldom responded to prospect objections or interpreted questions/obstacles as objections ☐

Business Knowledge

- Displayed understanding of business concepts through reflective comments, correct interpretation and relevant questions ☐
- Displayed understanding of business concepts only ☑   TALKED ABOUT PROSPECT'S BUSINESS, BUT DID NOT RELATE TO PROFIT MARGIN, ROI, OR BUSINESS GOALS.
- Displayed minimal understanding of business concepts ☐

Sales Presentations

- Well-organized and used effectively ☐   NOT USED AT THIS TIME.
- Not used effectively ☐
- Not well-organized ☐
- Seldom used at appropriate times ☐

Closing Skills

	TRIAL CLOSED THROUGHOUT
● Trial closed throughout. Used logical and assertive closing techiques to gain commitment	☑
● Assertively asked for the order/gained commitment. But no effective trial closes	☐
● Hesitated to ask for the order. Did not assertively gain commitment	☐

SOLUTION/SERVICE EVALUATION (EXAMPLE)

Account: _____ Contact: _____

Call objective: _____

FEATURE	BENEFIT	FEATURE	BENEFIT

COMMENTS

Objections
- Properly questioned, tested and overcame objections . . . . □
- Did not always properly question/test objections before overcoming them . . . . □
- Questioned/tested objections, but seldom overcame them effectively . . . . □

Sales Presentations
- ● Well-organized and used effectively . . . . □
- ● Not used effectively . . . . □
- ● Not well-organized . . . . □
- ● Seldom used at appropriate times . . . . □

Closing Skills
- ● Trial closed throughout. Used logical and assertive closing techiques to gain commitment . . . . □
- ● Assertively asked for the order/gained commitment. But no effective trial closes . . . . □
- ● Hesitated to ask for the order. Did not assertively gain commitment . . . . □

Oral Communication Skills
- ● Used precise expression in a clear, logical, conversational manner. Commanded attention and ensured understanding . . □
- ● Expressed ideas clearly, logically and concisely. But inadequ-ate articulation and/or inflection . . . . □
- ● Expressed ideas in a clear, logical manner, but rambled . . . . □
- ● Seldom expressed ideas in a concise manner with clarity and logic . . . . □

Organization

- Presented relevant features in a systematic order, according to the situation, criteria and interest .... ☐
- Presented features in a systematic order, but spent an inordinate time on those of little importance. .... ☐
- Jumped from feature to feature with little attention to the situation, criteria or interest .... ☐

Transitional Phrases (the demonstration, if appropriate)

- Throughout demonstration, used good terminology in progressing from feature to feature and criterion to criterion ... ☐
- Good terminology used between most features and criteria ... ☐
- Seldom used good terminology in progressing from point to point .... ☐

STEP EIGHT

ACCOUNT PLANNING – THE WORLD OF THE BIGGER DEAL

TIP *29* *The Environment*

A sale is an exchange. For the exchange to take place, certain conditions need to be fulfilled. There must be two parties, each of which must have something that may be of value to the other. Each party must be capable of communication and delivery, and free to accept or reject any offers made.

If these conditions exist, there is potential for exchange. Whether exchange actually takes place depends upon whether the two parties can find terms of exchange that leave them both better off than before the exchange. It is therefore a value-adding process whereby there is an act of free exchange which increases the value felt by both parties.

The fact that people have needs and wants, and that there are solutions and services that are capable of satisfying them, is necessary, but not sufficient, to define marketing. Marketing exists when people decide to satisfy their needs and wants in a certain way and that is called an exchange.

It is important to distinguish between selling and marketing and to define that bigger deal environment which you will find increasingly complex. Selling and marketing are often confused. Levitt confirms the contrast between the two when he says: 'Selling focuses on the needs of the seller; marketing on the needs of the buyer. Selling is preoccupied with the seller's need to convert products or services into cash; marketing with the idea of satisfying the needs of the customer . . .'

The whole concept of selling assumes that people and companies will not buy enough of your company's products and services unless they are approached with a substantial selling and promotional effort. The assumption is that your products and services are sold, not bought. Provided that customer satisfaction is not considered secondary to closing the sale, then trust between buyer and seller should exist.

But to achieve those bigger deals, you will need to adopt the tasks and philosophies of marketing – something best described as the determination of the needs, wants and values of your prospects. You will need to adapt in order to deliver those desired requirements more effectively and more efficiently than your competitors.

The larger and more complex the sale, the larger the perceived risk the buyer takes; the larger the marketing cycle; and the greater the competitive effort. Large accounts involve large numbers of people, and there is an increasing need to develop, and continue, a sound customer/prospect relationship based on trust. You may also face decentralization within your account, making an overview of your account more difficult. You may be helped, on the other hand, by the centralization of purchasing policies.

To become that true consultant to your customer's/prospect's business, you must become a business planner, a time manager and a business management strategist for both yourself and your account. Account planning is the primary method by which you make that transition. What large account salespeople are required to do is something that is initially alien to us all – PLAN. In the past, if we have done any planning at all, it has often been for leisure, not work. But in fact, we should plan our work and live our leisure – not vice versa.

For centuries, philosophers have implored us to plan our lives. But how can we, when we don't know what we want? Even when we do know, it is always subject to change. As a result, few of us have any perception as to how we can truly plan our lives.

Account planning in business is much simpler than planning your life. You can set objectives. Here, again, we often fail, usually for one of two basic reasons: we waste countless hours on documenting information on chosen accounts but little time in actually setting objectives; we 'profile' our account but do not 'plan the strategy'; we spend hours gleaning information, but then never use it! Or, we 'plan' a strategy for an account but don't dream of the potential that exists within it; so the strategies never reflect the true potential; we are afraid that if we document potential, our manager will simply raise our quotas or cut our territory.

There is no need for these attitudes. Managers tend not to believe ambitious plans and will leave territory and quota intact. Aim high: your plan will be much better. Is it not better to shoot at the moon and hit an eagle, than shoot at an eagle and hit a rock? If your goals are great, your plan to realize them will be great. As the elderly George Bernard Shaw told an audience, 'When I was young, I planned to spend two periods each week doing nothing but thinking. I never achieved my plan, but trying to has made me rich and famous'.

There is no conflict between your goal and your objective. The goal reflects the ideal, perfection. The objective is more practical in use, precise and measurable, being set in terms of the results to be achieved over a shorter period of time.

In the following planning guide, emphasis has been placed on those facets of the planning process that are the keys to successful account planning. In using this process, you'll become motivated to pursue the plan that you have developed. In addition, your support team will have a far clearer understanding of what you are trying to achieve, resulting in genuine teamwork.

T_{IP}30 *Now You Know Where, Why?*

The business climate is changing. In the past, you may have been successful in 'selling' your solutions and services, but now find that your company is unable to reach its revenue and profit objectives by adopting traditional selling approaches towards medium and large accounts.

When you consider the size of your market-place, the number of competent competitors and the objectives that any progressive company sets itself on a year-to-year basis, it becomes imperative for you to develop a strategy for marketing to large, key accounts, and to close those bigger deals.

Many salespeople who call on major accounts lack training, not only in planning but also in developing long-term strategies for account penetration. Account planning provides a means for assisting you in assessing the potential for your solutions and services in a given account, and converting that potential to orders. You need that planning process in order to obtain those good results, to protect your installed business and to close that incremental business. It's lengthy and mentally challenging work, requiring you to look at old problems in a new way.

Before you can penetrate that large account environment, you need to develop a consultative relationship with your account. Consultative selling requires in-depth knowledge of your prospects' businesses, objectives, plans and problems. Account planning provides that foundation for successful consultative selling.

When properly developed, this consultative relationship will prove the key to your future success in achieving your revenue objectives. In addition, you will develop a sound relationship that will help you to maintain not only your professional edge, but also leadership in your industry.

The alternative is simple: remain just another salesperson calling on the account, trying to sell a solution or service.

Remember, planning and operating a marketing plan are skills that can be learned and improved with practice. The purpose is not to create paperwork, but to help you run your accounts more effectively and improve your marketing position, relative to your competitors.

Account planning is an intensive, investigative process whereby a marketing team (or individual) develops a long-range marketing strategy for a specified account, producing a written account plan.

Aims

1) To develop a comprehensive understanding of your account's objectives and problems and increase the effectiveness of your marketing team, including your support personnel.
2) To develop a comprehensive long-range marketing plan for your account and make better use of available resources.
3) To develop a consultative relationship with your account.
4) To realize the full potential of the products and services you can offer your account and to exceed your targets.

Process

1) Collection and analysis of facts relating to your account's short- and long-range objectives, including the problems that both you and your account face in reaching these objectives.
2) Learning how your account operates and what areas affect the decisions made within the company. You need to consider the company's financial position, goals, organizational structure, informal power struc-

ture, personnel and marketing opportunities.

3) Building a model of your account, by establishment or department, in terms of influential people, organizational objectives, priorities, problems, people (decision-makers, recommenders, influencers), budget, space, trends and potential for your solutions and services.

Results

With in-depth account knowledge, you will develop a successful strategy to realize the full potential of your solution or service in your account. Knowing more about your account and its internal workings, you are in a good position to meet your account's objectives and to resolve their problems and needs. You will be in a position to present your solutions in terms that your account understands.

With this detailed information on you and your account now available, the benefits for you are significant. You will:

● Have greater control over those accounts that can make or break your quota
● Be better able to match your own and your support team's skills to the characteristics of your account
● Be able to negotiate, with your manager, real measurable objectives that will be challeng-

ing, yet realistic

- Be able to play an active part in the implementation of your plan, being an informed and true asset on key calls
- Be able to reduce losses in company productivity when you are promoted! The account plan that you have put in place will be an excellent vehicle for familiarizing your replacement with the account, strategy and marketing activity
- Be thoroughly prepared and able to react quickly as your company introduces new solutions and services or as your customers needs change
- Be able to keep your management informed and involved in your plans.

The benefits for your accounts are also significant. They will gain because:

- Their (and your) time is used more productively, owing to the fact that you are better informed and organized
- An improved perception and a greater trust will be developed
- Ultimately, they will buy solutions and services that really meet their needs and requirements.

The account planning journey you will make can be summarized as follows:

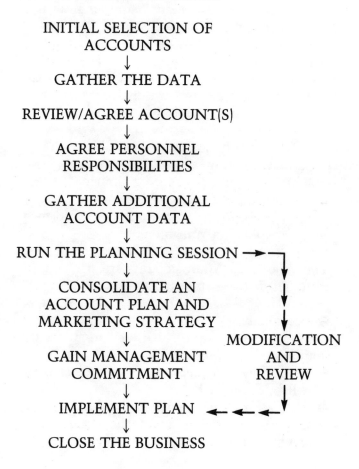

INITIAL SELECTION OF
ACCOUNTS
↓
GATHER THE DATA
↓
REVIEW/AGREE ACCOUNT(S)
↓
AGREE PERSONNEL
RESPONSIBILITIES
↓
GATHER ADDITIONAL
ACCOUNT DATA
↓
RUN THE PLANNING SESSION ──┐
↓   │
CONSOLIDATE AN   │
ACCOUNT PLAN AND   │
MARKETING STRATEGY   │
↓   MODIFICATION   │
GAIN MANAGEMENT   AND   │
COMMITMENT   REVIEW   │
↓   │
IMPLEMENT PLAN ◄ ◄ ◄ ──────┘
↓
CLOSE THE BUSINESS

TIP 33 *Make a Selection*

You should select the current major accounts which offer the greatest potential for incremental business, as well as large companies (or individuals) that you consider 'dormant'.

Invest your time where you think your return will be greatest. Determine the length of time that you consider reasonable to obtain results.

When selecting your account(s), and to determine the value of the account(s) you should consider the following questions:

● Do you and your company have a good rapport with the account?
● Is the account financially healthy and able to make investments?
● Have you identified individuals, areas or departments that show potential for your solutions and services?
● What use does the account currently make of your solutions and services?
● What has been your success to date in the account?
● If there are corporate headquarters, are they in your territory, and how strongly do they influence decisions?
● Is it a multi-locational account?
● Is the account one where you have traditionally not marketed to the potential available?

You should agree on your selected account within 30 days of drawing up your initial selection list. The objectives during this review are to gain a general overview of your selection and assess the potential for your solutions and services.

The initial effort of account planning should be directed at this review. Based on your data, certain accounts will be discarded for the purpose of full account planning. On those selected, you will be able to determine the direction for the planning session that follows. Knowing what to present simplifies the task of compiling the relevant information and, since the purpose of this review is effective communication, adequate preparation, completeness and logical organization will contribute to the effectiveness of your presentation.

Review outline
1) Data

● Introduce your account and name your account team (if appropriate). Include additional, but meaningful, information. An example might be the time that you have spent on the account to date.
● Provide an account description. This is general information about your account, such as:
  • Type of business
  • Types of solutions/services
  • Account's significance in its industry

- Size in relation to other similar organizations
- Number of locations
- Number of employees.

● Provide a general statement as to your perception of your account's problems and objectives. This could provide an insight into the direction that you might take in your marketing efforts.

● Outline your account's financial position. The annual report and articles in business and trade publications will provide a valuable insight as to how the senior management are running your major accounts.

● Provide an organization chart identifying decision-makers, recommenders and influencers.

● Provide information about the procedures in place for the acquisition of solutions and services. Explain, via the organizational data, who influences or reinforces purchasing decisions.

● Outline your company's record on installed solutions and services for the last three years. Describe your recent sales results for the current year. Determine future potential, direction and emphasis.

2) Marketing (general)

● Give a brief overview of your company's marketing position in your account. For example:

- Are you a major or minor vendor?
- Do you successfully market to all locations of your account?
- What is your marketing penetration?
- What are your management contact levels?
- Briefly state any problems that you currently face. This could, for example, relate to some of the items above or to other areas, such as:
  - A general lack of knowledge
  - Your account limiting your contacts to the purchasing department
  - Variable solution and service acceptance within departments of your account.
- Demonstrate an understanding of your account's senior management, company philosophy, etc, with emphasis on productivity, cost control, growth and profit.

3) Solution and service marketing

- Summarize the position of each of your solutions and services within the account. The primary areas of interest are:
  - Status (summarize the use and acceptability of your own solutions and services)
  - Competition (summarize the use and acceptability of competitive solutions and services)
  - Problems (summarize the most significant problems that you face in marketing your solutions and services)

- Objectives (outline those objectives which you can realistically expect to attain in both the short- and long-term).

4) Account potential

● The potential of your account is the actual revenue which you can realistically anticipate. To illustrate that potential, you should develop a three-year projection, based on your forecast.

5) Forecast

● Forecasts for your account, when your knowledge may be superficial, are obviously difficult. However, a consistency in presentation format of both current sales and your forecasts will simplify and promote an improved understanding of those reviewing your accounts.

6) Current marketing strategy

● Summarize the basic strategy and activities currently employed in your marketing to the account.

7) Current resources

● In addition to yourself, confirm any other resources that have been allocated to the account.

TIP 35 *Who Does What?*

Account planning is most effective when all the people involved in the account participate in the review and planning sessions. More dynamic planning results from the interaction of the participants, each serving as a catalyst to the other. It becomes even more successful with your management's participation, guidance and follow-up. You need to:

● Gather all necessary account information prior to the planning session
● Actively participate (lead) in the session
● Determine the account plan
● Present and gain agreement to your plan from management
● Implement and actively pursue your plan
● Schedule monthly reviews
● Keep management aware of your progress
● Update your plan as necessary.

Your manager needs to:

● Approve the account(s) suggested for formal account planning (at the initial account review)
● Prioritize the accounts in order of importance
● Ensure that all pre-meeting activities are completed
● Receive the formal presentation of the account plan

- Make appropriate suggestions for improving the plan
- Approve the account plan and objectives
- Actively support implementation of the plan
- Provide and help secure additional resources where requested
- Review monthly against the plan.

STEP NINE

ACCOUNT PLANNING – GETTING DOWN TO IT

$T_{IP}36$ _What are You Trying to Do?_

The objectives of an account planning session are to develop an account plan for XYZ company (or an individual). This plan will be measurable, time-targeted and attainable (though challenging). It should help you to:

● Exceed quota/targets
● Develop new opportunities/achieve potential
● Increase your effectiveness
● Make better use of your company's valuable resources.

Sample agenda for an account planning session
1) Introduction
   • Objectives
   • Explanation of the principles of planning and principles for the session
   • Explanation of the ground-rules for the session
2) Account environment
   • Account's viewpoint
   • Work requirement
   • Our capabilities
3) Account information
   • Account description
   • Financial position
   • Organization/power structure
   • Personnel profiles
   • Purchasing procedures
4) Assumptions
5) Account position

6) Competition
   - Level of acceptance
7) Opportunities
   - By establishment/department/individual
8) Marketing objectives
9) Marketing problems
10) Solutions
11) Marketing action plans
12) Assessment of the session

In the first instance, the planning session involves learning how your account operates, its organization, its goals, its concerns and its financial position. In other words, you first need to understand and establish the environment of your account. With this in-depth knowledge, you can then establish your marketing objectives and define any problems preventing you from reaching those objectives. Your next assignment is to determine the solutions to those problems and, finally, to develop a strategy and a time-action plan for carrying them out.

The account planning session is an extension of the account review, where accounts are considered for full account planning, but goes into considerably greater detail. All information gathered for the initial account review will be put to good use during the full planning session.

The plan that you develop at this stage will not be cast in concrete; it will be continually reviewed and modified to meet the changing needs, not only of your own company, but also of your account. *Planning is an on-going activity.*

With the increasing complexity of your products and services, aggressive quotas and targets, and an increase in competitive activity, the need for well-developed marketing strategies is clear. Your major accounts offer your greatest potential and your greatest exposure.

The General Principles

Without question, major account planning is vital to your and your company's success in the future.

The Planning Session – Basic Principles

For a really effective planning session, the following basic principles must be borne in mind:

● *You are all peers*: everyone has an equal voice and an equal vote on the issues raised. Everyone's opinions count.

● *There is no time limit*: any stated timings are for guidance only. You cannot be creative with a time limit. Time limits tend to reinforce the old way of viewing the problem.

● *Any invited management must operate the two-thirds rule*: two-thirds of the time when they want to say something, they should keep quiet! What you need are *your* perspectives and experience. The action plan that you will develop is your plan, not your manager's plan – you're the one who has to make it work.

● *The session must start promptly*: break times must be observed; all participants are expected to stay for the entire session – no late arrivals or early departures.

● *There should be no interruptions*: such as telephone calls or unplanned visitors.

● *Planning is valuable*: there is a bridge at Avignon in France which is only half a bridge. It looks like it might have been bombed during the war. But it wasn't. Three hundred years ago, the people of Avignon decided that they needed a bridge across the Rhone river, so they started to build one.

They arrived at mid-stream and found that the riverbed was sand and therefore unable to support a bridge. In many companies, you'll find such 'half-built' bridges owing to a tendency to *re*activity rather than *pro*activity. Account planning makes you build your plan on bedrock, by clearly establishing objectives with an associated plan.

TIP 39 Structure

During the planning session, no one should be told what to do and how to do it. This is called an heuristic approach, the objective being to establish some basic guidelines and then, through trial and error, to achieve an action plan to which you are all totally committed. As there may be 'pain' in its creation, this commitment will be 100 per cent! Mistakes will be made and some work may have to be re-done, but you cannot teach anyone to think – you have to learn on your own.

Here are the ground-rules of the planning session:

● **Think**: it's hard work, as well as being frustrating, but you must force yourself to use all your creativity and imagination, looking at things in a new way. Einstein said that imagination was more important than knowledge. Typically, you have account knowledge, but now you must use that information, together with your imagination to achieve your objectives. Archaeologists dig around for hours to find small bones, perhaps a shinbone here or a molar there. Using imagination, they come up with a complete description of a giant dinosaur, together with its sex, age, height, width and what it ate for lunch. With a few clues and logical assumptions, you can develop a similarly detailed understanding of your account as well.

● **Think in specifics**: this aids clear and precise

thinking. No vague or general statements should be accepted. Everything should be reduced to specifics. Things are important or they are not important. You cannot plan with 'maybes'.

● **Don't duck issues:** you must deal with them one at a time, resolving each before you move onto another. No matter how difficult the problem, you must resolve it to everyone's satisfaction before you tackle another. Watch out for general statements or compromises for the sake of finishing, and also for sudden changes in positions.

● **Insist on 100 per cent agreement:** participants must not be forced into accepting a position that they do not really support. Plans do not work if people are not committed, and there won't be commitment unless there is consensus. The key is to make sure that you understand others' positions before you defend your own.

● **Use simple, complete sentences:** this will keep your thinking clear as well as precise. While it's considered fashionable to 'net things out', this is often done at the expense of the real meaning of the point. If it's not lost in five minutes, it's certainly lost by the next day. As your plan will be reviewed and updated, it's important that you discipline yourself to simple and complete sentences.

It has been found that the most productive

number of participants in a session is between three and six. This size of group generates the most effective group dynamics.

Participants should include the account manager, appropriate supporting staff and marketing management. In complex account planning sessions, 'moderators' should be involved, chosen from respected and experienced members of your company, who are not involved in your account. Their objectives are:

● To keep all the participants on track
● To request clarification
● To suggest alternatives
● To channel and control the discussion
● To motivate people to actively participate.

Whatever plan is developed, it must be one that the team has developed itself. It must be a plan in which the team has confidence, and to which they are all totally committed.

TIP*40*   *Account Environment*

Aim
To determine what is known about the account in terms of the account's viewpoint and requirements, then to determine how you can address those requirements.

Overview
You will need a detailed description of the following topics, built on the data that you collected for the initial review and selection of accounts:

- *Account's viewpoint*: determine your account's viewpoint in terms of where they're going in the areas of your solutions and services as well as your own ability to assist them in getting there. In addition, confirm their overall goals. For broad objectives, these could be, for example, profit, return to shareholders and social responsibility. Specific objectives may include cost control.
- *Work requirement*: determine your account's requirements at each of the levels in which you perceive your solutions or services have a 'fit'. As an example, you might take the levels of junior, middle and executive management.
- *Your capabilities*: having identified your account's work requirements, ask yourself the question, 'What solutions and services does my company actually possess that would address the requirements at each level?'.

TIP*41* *Account Information*

Aim
To determine what is known about your
account in terms of business/industry organization, organizational structure and background.

Overview
This section requires a detailed description of
your account. Again, you will be building on
the data that you collected for your initial
review and selection of accounts. The description must include:

● The industry
● Major solutions and services
● Number of employees
● Geographic location
● Financial position (which may include:
  • Gross sales
  • Earnings
  • Sales or income growth rates
  • Profit margins
  • Price earnings ratios
  • Capital expenditures
  • Yields
  • Dividends)
● Organization chart/power structure includ-
  ing:
  • Key decision-makers
  • Recommenders and influencers
  • Major departments/divisions
  • Number of employees in each depart-
    ment/division

- Types of solutions and services used in each department/division
- Personnel profiles. Identify key decision-makers and people within the 'informal' power structure. Indicate your highest level of contact and how well you know him or her. Then build a personality model of these individuals according to:

  - Age
  - Time with company
  - Position
  - Time in present position
  - Major goals and concerns
  - Attitude towards your company*
  - How well you know the individual**
  - Their level of influence
  - Hobbies and leisure pursuits
  - If a decision-maker, who influences and how strongly?

  *Good – Fair – Receptive – Unreceptive
  **Use scale of 1–5 (Know very well – don't know at all)

Note: We have all missed this key step – targeting the decision-maker – on more than one occasion! To implement a successful account plan, you must know who the key decision-maker is, but realize that no one makes that decision alone. You will have people around you who are prime influencers of your proposal – at all levels of your account's management structure. You must sell to all people involved in the process, appealing to each individual in terms of their niche in your account. All too often, you may be convinced that position alone dictates an individual's power in your account. However, if you think about it, you can easily find examples that challenge that perception:

- Managing director approves orders. But not interested in making decisions because he or she is due to retire in six months.
- Director of finance exerts strong power in your account and no decisions are made without his or her concurrence. Yet, there is great reliance on the director of marketing, who he or she perceives will be the next managing director. His or her boss!
- The marketing director never makes any decisions without the involvement of the financial controller and a cash-flow analysis.

Important people will always take time for important things. In a large account, however, seldom does anyone make decisions against the advice of people on whom they rely.

- Purchasing procedures. Outline the procedures, however complex. Include:
  - Date that operating budgets are submitted

- Budget approval process
- Financial year
- Individual or departmental approval of budgets
- Individual or departmental approval of specifications
- Individual or departmental budget limits.

Outline how your solutions or services are typically bought by your account. Define the paperwork flow from internal financial request to purchase order.

TARGET THE DECISION-MAKERS PROCESS

```
┌──────────────────────────────────────────┐
│        INFLUENCERS OF INFLUENCERS         │
│   ┌──────────────────────────────────┐    │
│   │         PRIME INFLUENCERS         │    │
│   │   ┌──────────────────────────┐    │    │
│   │   │                          │    │    │
│   │   │         DECISION          │    │    │
│   │   │          MAKER            │    │    │
│   │   │                          │    │    │
│   │   └──────────────────────────┘    │    │
│   │         PRIME INFLUENCERS         │    │
│   └──────────────────────────────────┘    │
│        INFLUENCERS OF INFLUENCERS         │
└──────────────────────────────────────────┘
```

Decision-makers never make decisions without support.

Prime influencer may not be in your account. Could be outside consultant or managing director of a subsidiary, for example.

Sales efforts should be directed to selfish interests. Marketing reasons to marketing, financial reasons to finance.

Aim
To consider your account's current plans and to determine which of these plans may affect your position in the account.

Overview
You should make certain assumptions about your account based on what is known of the current situation. You should consider the changes that you believe will take place and why current trends are apparent in your account. Before determining what significant effect these events could have on your own company, you must assess the validity of the assumptions within the following categories:

- *Expected change:* identify possible organizational change, such as:
  - Who is being groomed for that top slot?
  - Are there other changes in key personnel?
  - Is there an apparent power play within the decision-making body?
  - Are there positions being eliminated or added?
  - Are departments being created?

- *Company policy:* consider any changes in company policy, such as:
  - Employee benefits
  - Hiring policy
  - Purchasing

● *Current trends:* determine what appear to be current trends, such as:
  - Growth or expansion
  - Decentralization
  - Creation of autonomous units
  - Young management moving into key positions
  - Progressive, innovative management
  - Positive approach to education
  - Relationships with competitors

TIP 43 *Account Position*

Aim

To identify your company's inventory/revenue in your account.

Overview

This section requires a detailed description of 'installed' solutions and services from your company. A three-year sales history should be available, including a year-to-date position.

You should have available your current year's forecast by solution and service as well as anticipated revenue.

Aim

To identify your competitors' installed solutions and services, and confirm their activity. Answer the question, 'Do you have the capability to do the job better?' Determine any advantages that your competitor possesses. Define any competitive advantage that you need to develop and the date by which you need to develop it.

Overview

This section requires a detailed description of installed competitive solutions and services as well as your answer to the question above. You should understand if there is one significant competitor or many. In all cases, you should have an understanding of the last three years' sales history, as well as of their latest proposals in the account.

TIP45 *Now's Your Chance!*

Aim
Identify areas of your major account which could provide opportunities for your solutions and services.

Overview
Determine which specific areas within your account offer the best potential for your solutions and services, and develop a model of these areas including:

- Establishment/department heads, recommenders and influencers concerned
- Establishment/department structure
- Objectives
- Problems and concerns
- Trends, changes
- Budget
- Competitive products.

Identify priority areas within the total organization, or in specific areas, on which you could have an effect. Typical programmes might be:

- Cost-effectiveness
- Job enrichment
- Customer satisfaction.

TIP46 *Set Those Goals*

Aim

Answer the question, 'What do you want to accomplish in this account, both in the short- and long-term?' Your objectives should address the real potential in your account, not just what is possible at this time or in the next six months.

Overview

You must develop marketing objectives that are measurable, time-targeted, challenging yet attainable.

A gross list of objectives should be agreed. Broad, immeasurable 'goals' should then be eliminated or re-stated as objectives. Generally, the majority of objectives will be short-term (six months) in nature although you must draw up those longer-term objectives that relate to the potential within your account. You should then prioritize this list of objectives.

Also ask yourself, 'Is there any other information that must be validated before I develop my complete strategy?'

Aim

Determine your perception as to the obstacles that might prevent you from meeting your marketing objectives. What is the nature of each problem? Is it significant? Is it solvable? Problems may well be account-orientated, such as poor facilities, lack of controls, financial concerns, the standard of personnel or internal, political considerations. On the other hand, they may relate to problems generated by your own company such as lack of support, inefficient billing systems or poor response times. Determine which are fact and which are assumptions, and prioritize these identified problems.

Overview

This section requires the development of a prioritized list of problems. Ask the question, 'Which problems do I face that hinder the attainment of my marketing objectives?' The resulting list should then be analyzed with the problems being defined more specifically in terms of cause and effect. The intention is to get to the real root cause. A prioritization of this newly-defined list should then be made, with each problem relating directly to a specific marketing objective.

Do not discuss solutions yet.

TIP48 *You've Got the Answer*

Aim
Answer the question, 'What must I do to achieve my objectives and minimize, or eliminate, my problems?'

Overview
Address the objectives first. As action plans are developed for these objectives, many problems will be resolved as well. Objectives should be handled one at a time, and specific activities to accomplish them considered without concern for priority, completion dates, responsibility or necessary resources.

There must be agreement that your solutions are realistic before tackling the next objective or problem.

TIP 49
Make Sure Your Answer Works

Aim

Finalize your marketing strategy for each of your company's solutions and services, preparing a timetable of activities.

Overview

This section requires a detailed description of your marketing strategy for each of your solutions and services as well as specific action plans in terms of who is responsible for what, by when and how it will be accomplished. A contingency plan should be prepared for unexpected situations or in case planned events do not take place.

You should complete a marketing forecast, based upon your agreed strategy, by solution and service potential.

A test of 'reasonableness' confirms the commitment to the plan. Each person writes down his/her commitments from the action plan and checks them against his/her diary. If there are no obvious conflicts, scheduled reviews of the progress of the plan's implementation can now be formally scheduled.

TIP 50 *How Well Did You Do?*

To test the effectiveness of the session, ask the following questions:

● Is the account's environment adequately identified and understood?
● Are your problems explicitly and succinctly defined?
● Do you have a clear understanding of your competitor's activity?
● Are your objectives:
  • Realistic
  • Explicit
  • Attainable (but challenging)
  • Measurable?
● How will the plan be monitored and maintained and who has that responsibility?

T_IP51 *Watch Out!*

There may, of course, be pitfalls in the account planning process. Whenever a group of people is involved in any type of discussion and problem solving activity, there is every possibility that any of the following situations could develop. It's important that you are particularly sensitive to these situations and attempt to prevent or resolve them quickly, so that they do not impede the progress of your plan. Pitfalls might include:

● Personality clashes
● Participants being concerned that they are being 'evaluated' during the meetings
● Presence of a non-participant – a person who is not motivated to contribute
● One or two members 'taking over' and forcing their views on others
● An experienced person refusing to take a fresh look at alternatives
● Lack of total agreement
● Too many assumptions being made without proper validation
● Participants rushing through the process or becoming bogged down with one item
● Participants starting to design solutions too early
● A plan that's too ambitious
● The injection of too much formality, restraining creativity
● Poor account selection
● Over-optimism

Watch Out!

● Over-cautiousness
● Attempting too much in too short a time
● Failure to revise, refine and replan
● Objectives not reflecting customer needs
● You losing control.

STEP TEN

ACCOUNT PLANNING – DOING WHAT YOU SAID YOU'D DO

T_{IP}52 *Implementing Your Plan*

A good plan will serve as a point of reference for maintaining priorities on a day-to-day basis. Do not put it in a file and forget it – the many hours spent gathering data and planning will then have been little more than a paperwork exercise.

One problem that you may have faced in the planning session is a lack of accurate and current account records. However, once you have completed your account plan, it should serve as the focal point for assembling a database on your account.

As you carry out your planned activities, new information will become available. Some problems will be resolved, others will arise. As usual, whatever else happens, the one certain thing that will occur will be change.

Use your plan as your guide, adapting to the changes, yet keeping the agreed goals and objectives in mind.

TIP53 *Did You Get it Right?*

The cumulative effect of the accomplishment of your major marketing objectives, together with unforeseen problems, are two good reasons for reviewing and modifying your account plan.

The extent of your review will depend on your current familiarity with your account and the perceived degree of modification required.

You should give consideration to the following:

- Attainment to date
- Significant sales and other successes
- Accomplishment of objectives
- Changes in priorities
- Use of support staff
- Recommendations for change (targets and assigned budgets).

TIP54

So, You Really had a Good Account Plan?

The following is a list of strategy-probing questions which you should use during your account plan review to assess validity and completeness. These questions may also be used by your account team to stimulate fresh thinking in any modification of the account plan.

'Applications' (of solution/service)
1) Which major 'application' areas does your plan address?
2) What is the process used by your account to identify and justify 'applications' and how are you involved in it?
3) How can your company's total organization and offerings be incorporated in your account plan?
4) How much does your account currently spend on competitive solutions and/or services, and why?

Offerings
1) What does your account believe are the benefits and financial justification of its installed and 'on order' solutions/services purchased from you?
2) What competitive solutions and/or services is your account looking at and for what reasons?
3) Is your plan consistent with your account's perception of a 'perfect' world as related to your company's offerings?

4) Are there any obstacles preventing you from meeting your account objectives? If so, what will you do to overcome them?

5) What resources are needed from your company to help you meet your account's objectives?

Implementation of your solution/service

1) How does your account measure the effectiveness of your solution/service? What are your plans to improve it?

2) Which user executives are unhappy with your solution/service? Why?

3) How does your account forecast product/service requirements?

4) What is your understanding of your account's requirements for the next 12 months? What is the ability of your company to meet these requirements?

Acquisition

1) Given your account's financial position, policies and plans, what specific financial implications must your proposal address?

2) Which of your account's executives must review and approve your proposals? What are their attitudes?

3) If your account had informed you that it had received a proposal to replace your installed and on order solutions/services at a higher cost, how would you respond?

4) What alternatives are your competitors

likely to recommend?

5) Does your account quantify and include your company's added value when making supplier decisions?

Executive marketing

1) How does your plan support your account's objectives?

2) What key organizational and management changes do you anticipate in the next two years and how would these changes affect your plans?

3) What are the weaknesses in your account that a competitor might exploit? If none, how will your account react to competitive price decreases?

4) What would be the impact on your plan if your key supporter (within your account) left?

5) Suppose a consultant was engaged to evaluate your account's plan as it related to your solutions/services. Do you feel confident about the validity of your current plan?

6) What are your plans to encourage a strong partnership between your account's executives and your company?

7) What are the major added-value contributions that your company has provided to your account in the last 12 months? Has your account's top management perceived that value? If so, what is it? If not, how do you plan to communicate added value to

your account's top management? What major added-value contributions are you planning?

8) Which aspects of your plan do you intend to discuss with your account?

9) Why does your account do business with you?

STEP ELEVEN

DECISION-MAKING –
ARE YOU GOOD AT IT?

TIP 55 *Questionnaire*

Complete this questionnaire.

1) How would you describe your problem-solving and decision-making abilities?

Highly analytical	Highly creative
Moderately analytical	Moderately creative
Occasionally analytical	Occasionally creative
Rarely analytical	Rarely creative

2) How often are your problems and decision-making situations described by the following?

	Most of the time			Very rarely
Difficult or complex	5	4	3	2	1
Ill-defined or 'fuzzy'	5	4	3	2	1
Binary (either/or) choice	5	4	3	2	1
High Impact to you or others	5	4	3	2	1
High risk to you or others	5	4	3	2	1

3) How often do you do the following when faced with a problem?

Separate the problem into single issues?	5	4	3	2	1
Prioritize the issues?	5	4	3	2	1
Explicitly list criteria for making a decision?	5	4	3	2	1

Explicitly list decision alternatives	5	4	3	2	1
Develop more than two alternatives before deciding	5	4	3	2	1
Explicitly list the risks of a decision alternative?	5	4	3	2	1

4) How easy do you find the following tasks?

	Very easy				Very difficult
Determining root problems of complex problems	5	4	3	2	1
Expanding the list of possible alternatives you can take	5	4	3	2	1
Perceiving the risks inherent in making a decision	5	4	3	2	1
Making a decision the first time and sticking to it	5	4	3	2	1

5) What skills are you interested in using more often in your problem-solving and decision-making activities?

	Very interested				Not at all interested
Sorting out complex problems	5	4	3	2	1
Determining the root causes of problems	5	4	3	2	1

Expanding the selection of decision alternatives	5	4	3	2	1
Developing a system of choosing between alternatives	5	4	3	2	1
Developing the ability to anticipate risks in a decision	5	4	3	2	1

6) Would you like to be:
- More qualified in making decisions?
- More creative?

Read on!

TIP 56 *An Introduction*

To be an effective decision-maker, you need to be a creative thinker. And by creative thinker, I mean one who has the ability to alternate between divergent and convergent thinking. Divergent thinking involves using your imagination to create many different ideas. Convergent thinking means using your judgment to narrow down all the possibilities and select the best ideas.

True creativity comes from alternating between divergent and convergent thinking. It is not a frivolous activity. While it may not immediately provide practical solutions, it will be the source of some excellent ideas. You must be expressive – with quantity of ideas, rather than quality, being the initial goal. Judgment will come later. There are, however, many internal and external factors which can hamper this creativity, and you should obviously try to avoid these while generating ideas. Curbs to creativity include:

● Feeling embarrassed
● Habit
● Prejudice and preconceived ideas
● Lack of effort
● Negative attitudes (internal)
● Organizational structures
● Different environments
● Existing management attitudes
● Time constraints (external).

Remember that while you are generating all your ideas you must defer judgment. Every decision you make, however small, should:

● Use divergent and convergent thinking
● Use your good judgment to determine how deeply you should analyze the available information
● Use over-analysis if you are not experienced as you will tend to under-analyze.

TIP 57 *Did You Know?*

Common pitfalls of decision-making are:

- Failing to be specific (in identifying problems)
- Under-analyzing the available information
- Over-analyzing the available information
- Jumping to conclusions
- Solving symptoms instead of causes
- Reliance on 'hip-shooting'
- Considering only the first idea that comes to mind
- Paralysis, through fear of making a mistake
- Failure to anticipate risk
- Focusing on contingencies rather than on preventative actions
- Failure to consider opportunities.

TIP 58 *The Can of Worms*

Identifying problems is like dealing with the proverbial can of worms when fishing. You spread them out, separate them, select the fattest and leave the others.

Good decision-makers have the same discipline. They have the ability to sort out the urgent and important issues rather than tackling the entire 'bag of worms'. Problems come in different forms and you may not find it easy to focus on the specific nature of each problem you face. Often, what seems straightforward turns out to be complex and far-reaching.

You may be in the habit of using convenient labels for problems: 'the budget problem', 'the administrative problem'. You must resist the habit. If you label like this, all the issues get lumped together and confused. Successful decision-makers have the knack of sorting out this confusion in order to arrive at the essential issues.

To identify those issues, you must:

● Separate the confusion into single problems
  • What's the problem?
  • How does the problem manifest itself?
  • What are the elements of the problem?
  • What factors are contributing to the confusion?
● Clarify which of the elements are symptoms and which are effects
  • Write down the specific problem
● Establish which of these problems have

priority, based on the following criteria:
- Level of impact or seriousness
- Urgency.

Having established which of your problems have priority, you must:

● Clarify the cause
● Make a decision.

The following chart can help you develop and organize the facts about a problem that will lead you to possible causes. It can also provide an excellent base for testing possible causes.

	ACTUAL FACTS	**COMPARABLE FACTS**
WHO	What object, objects, individual or group's behaviour is a problem?	Which comparable object, objects, individuals or groups do not display this problem behaviour?

The Can of Worms

WHAT   *Problem is:*
What specific
problem
behaviour is
observed or
reported?

Problem is not:
What other
problem
behaviour might
be displayed by
this object or
individual, but
are not?

WHERE In what place is
this problem
behaviour
observed?

Where else might
the behaviour
occur, but does
not?

WHEN   *First:*
When was the
problem first
observed?
Since:
What has been
the history of
recurrence?

When has the
problem
behaviour not
occurred?

**HOW
MUCH**   *Numbers:*
How frequent is
the problem
behaviour?
How would you
quantify the
problem?

How frequent
might it be, but it
is not?
What comparable
quantities are not
observed?

Trend:
What is the trend?   What other trend might exist, but does not?

To identify possible causes, ask yourself:

● How do the problem's actual facts differ from the comparable, or 'non-problem', facts?
● What changes are associated with these differences? If the change occurred after the problem appeared, it cannot be relevant to the problem. If the change occurred long before, it may not be relevant.
● What possible causes do these differences and changes suggest?

What allows you to say, 'I made a good decision'? The chances are that it was for two reasons:

● The establishment of criteria
● The consideration of the risks

Example case

Situation: You must find a location for a company dinner.

Statement of the problem: Where will you hold this company dinner?

Pertinent facts: 50 people and £40/person (£2000).

The statement of the problem does not automatically limit your decision alternatives to restaurants. You can therefore be creative. It also has some applied assumptions: that the dinner will occur; that, as it is a dinner, it will be held on personal time.

In order to determine as to whether an alternative meets your requirements, you will need some criteria. To generate these criteria will require you to think divergently – in other words, for you to use your imagination. The criteria you generate should cover all the important factors because their consideration is crucial to your making a good decision the first time. In this example, 'drawing-out' questions might include:

● What would the ideal choice be?
● What things are essential?

● What limitations are imposed on me? Policies, for example.

Your criteria should be:

● The result that you want to achieve: each criterion should be unique and essential
● The simplest of statements: avoid criteria in a statement using 'and'
● Recognition of the constraints that you must live within.

You now need to judge your criteria – to place a value on them. While you used divergent thinking for the criteria determination, you would now use convergent thinking – using your judgment – to place that value. Ask yourself:

● Which criteria are absolutely essential?
● Which are significant enough to include?
● For your other criteria, what is their relative weight on a scale of 1 – 10 (10 being the highest):

Typically, you will develop a list of four to seven important criteria. Those with low weights will tend to be eliminated.

The need for exactness is a function of how critical your decision is: the more critical your decision, the more exact you need to be.

Alternatives now need to be created, deferring judgments until later. One of the most common failures in decision-making is not developing enough alternatives to give you the opportunity to make the best decision the first time. All too often, you jump at the first or most obvious thing that comes to mind. You always give yourself the chance of making the best decision when you have many alternatives from which to select.

Sometimes, the selection of the alternative will be obvious. Buf if it is not, you must compare your alternatives against your criteria. By doing this, your absolute criteria will act as the first screens to filter out unsuitable alternatives. Remaining alternatives are then compared to your relative criteria.

You must now assess the risks associated with your high-value alternatives. Ask yourself: What makes you feel uneasy about an alternative? What might go wrong? What requires close attention to make this alternative work? You are assessing the probability of the risk occurring and the seriousness of its impact.

If the risks are too serious for the primary alternative, you may want to reconsider your choice, especially if other alternatives are close in value. Test your decision against 'gut feel'. Think what you would do if your primary alternative failed this instinct test.

In order to bring a topic into focus and identify areas of weak thinking, you need to question. You will be able to determine how well an individual, as well as yourself, has thought through the available information; the manner in which they have focused on the data; and whether to probe for more specific content.

Try these questions on your colleagues and yourself in identifying problems:

- What is the concern?
- What it is that suggests something has gone wrong?
- What are some examples?
- What do you mean by . . . ?
- What are the elements that make up this concern?
- Are any of these problems interdependent?
- Which of these problems are the most serious? The most urgent?
- Do you know the cause of this problem?
- Which of these issues require a decision?

STEP TWELVE

EFFECTIVE PRESENTATIONS

TIP *61* *What and When*

There are four basic types of presentation:

- **Informational.** The main purpose here is to inform your audience about a particular topic. Tends to be relatively low-key in that you are not expecting a firm commitment to buy your solution at this time.

- **Selling.** Sales-orientated and should be well-prepared and organized. Can be supportive to a concurrent demonstration. Focuses on your prospect's agreed requirements and needs and how they will be addressed by your proposal.

- **Cost justification.** Typically, financial overview of the costs and benefits associated with your proposal.

- **Executive or Closing.** Used when meeting with executive management to review projects or to seek approval to your proposal. As a result, it should be the most professional of all your presentations. Practise, practise, to get this one right!

These different types of presentation are used in different phases of the Practical Selling Cycle. This summary should not be considered as a hard and fast set of rules. As long as you are aware of the different types of presentation, you can then apply your judgment in deciding when to use a particular presentation to support your selling campaign.

TIP 62 *Structure*

In preparing for any presentation, there is a simple, yet very useful structure for preparing a presentation message:

PROSPECT NEED → PROSPECT ADVANTAGES → YOUR PROPOSAL → YOUR ACTION

PROSPECT NEED

To truly communicate, you must consider your prospect's views. Every prospect has a need and nothing gains your prospect's attention faster than showing that you understand his or her problems and can help solve them. Need consists of two parts: symptoms and causes. In your calls, you will be identifying need through determining your prospect's 'hot spots' – symptoms. You will be speaking to your prospect's problems and experiences. You will then identify what you believe to be the major cause of those symptoms.

PROSPECT ADVANTAGES

There are two parts to the prospect advantages step: the main advantage and the added advantage. The main advantage demonstrates how your ideas will meet the need and resolve your prospect's problems. The added advantages are powerful persuaders that explain why your ideas are superior and compelling. Advantage statements should be specific.

YOUR PROPOSAL

You will often fail to communicate because you assume that your audience is as informed as you are about the topic. This is often the case where you have been involved in a lengthy sales campaign and make the assumption that you have already covered the benefits and advantages in previous meetings.

To make sure that your audience fully understands your proposal, you need to define it by explaining the general pattern. Then select details that clarify the pattern to the extent that your audience needs in order for them to understand the message.

YOUR ACTION

The action step consists of two parts: present and future. The present action is a single, immediate action that your audience must take to initiate the process (example: approve the order!). The future action will be a series of actions, spread out over a period of time (example: inform departments of order, form consultative groups, finalize policy, implement policy).

Your ideal presentation will cover the above four steps. You may change the position of the two parts – need and advantages, and proposal and action – according to your audience. Audiences with a sales viewpoint will usually respond to need and advantages followed by proposal and action. Those with a technical background may prefer the reverse.

Your ideal presentation will also make sure that the same four elements are clear, not only to you, but also to your audience. The message is now 'ours', not 'yours' or 'mine'.

The following format for presenting your proposal will help you connect with your audience. It will ensure that your presentation is forceful and compact, and give you control over the content and structure of your message. Adapt the elements so that they can be used in any sequence to fit your presentation agenda and to match your different audiences.

- Opening
  - Introduce yourself
  - Thank your prospects for their time
  - Build credibility
  - State your objectives
  - Confirm level of commitment you expect
  - Overview of events
- Agenda
  - Topics to be covered
- Overview
  - Brief presentation of your prospect's goals and objectives
  - The primary goals that you will address
- Review requirements
  - Those identified and agreed at prior discussions

● Proposal discussion (your solution)
  ● Highlight features and associated advantages, relating them to your prospect's needs and wants
● Benefits
  ● Translation of advantages into actual prospect benefits
● Close
  ● Summarize topics
  ● Outline your action plan – what you want your prospects to do based on what you have just told them.

Your message is the core of your presentation. This is where you must be your most persuasive. Persuasion is defined as causing someone to do something by argument, reasoning or entreaty. Most persuasion requires some form of evidence and, by understanding how your prospect processes information, you can relate the evidence required by his or her decision-making process.

Prospects process information in two ways: by *responding emotionally to imagery*, and by *using logic* to respond to such things as numerical calculations and organizing items in sequence. During your presentation, your audience will make decisions based upon these two ways of processing information. As a result, you must address these ways of perceiving information by: *appealing to imagery and appealing to logic*.

Ideally, the two ways of processing will reinforce each other, providing your audience with a powerful motivation to take action. As a result, to support your message in business presentations, use analogies to appeal to imagery and facts and figures to appeal to logic.

You will never be able to control your audience's feelings and actions. But you can plant images that create feelings that lead to actions. An analogy is one means by which you can plant that image in your audience's minds. An analogy is a type of comparison, the most effective drawing a comparison between two dissimilar things. It often appeals to common sense, a sense of humour and/or general human experience.

The analogy is probably the least used form of evidence and yet it is the most powerful. This is because it is creative and can prove your theory or principle both quickly and clearly. To make best use of it, you must step outside the environment of the subject. Sport, for instance, offers excellent opportunities to develop analogies, but you should select appropriate analogies that will elicit the kinds of feelings that will lead your prospects to the desired actions.

Appealing to your audience's logic you can take three forms – facts, stories and numbers (data). Facts include basic and accepted truths in our day-to-day business. Stories contain cases, examples and anecdotes. They are concrete, specific and credible. But they are specific to one time, place or person and do not necessarily transfer to others. Numbers consist of quantitative and statistical data. They transfer from one context to another and give a general idea of range and scope, but are not always interesting and may be hard to understand out of context. Statistics are the most frequently used form of evidence, though many people are suspicious of them. For this reason, it is always important to clearly state the source of statistics.

You should also note that the positive points of using stories tend to balance the negative points of using numbers and vice versa:

- *The Law of Variety:* to achieve balance in your presentation, for every set of numbers, tell a story. For every story, give a set of numbers.
- *The Law of Stinginess:* give facts and figures only for points that your audience doubt.
- *Use Auxillary Laws:* present one point at a time. Prove one point at a time. Use only the most powerful of facts and figures.

There are two other forms of 'evidence' that need to be mentioned: *experience* (both your own and your prospect's), and the *opinions of experts*. The use of expert opinions enables you to introduce objective credibility. It is advisable to use experts outside your own company. When using experts, state clearly who they are, along with their credentials.

TIP 64 *It's How You Say It*

There are many characteristics of effective verbal delivery. There are also some characteristics that will detract from effective delivery during a presentation. Some characteristics of effective verbal delivery are:

● **Vocabulary.** Your presentation should be geared to your audience. Therefore, use familiar terminology and acronyms which will not lose your prospects.

● **Voice level.** Sufficient for all to hear. Speaking loud and clearly is a simple way of ensuring that your prospects get your message. But be sure to combine that louder voice with projection and large descriptive gestures.

● **Inflection.** Changes in the pitch or tone of your voice add interest to your presentation. They can be used to highlight or emphasize points of interest. Use verbal variety: soft then loud; loud then soft.

● **Fluency.** You should know where you are going and be confident in the message that you are presenting. The overall flow and pace of your presentation should be smooth.

● **Attitude.** The confidence that you display will usually make or break your presentation. Confidence is displayed in the words that you use and the way in which you use your voice.

● **Audience sensitivity.** A good presenter is always aware of his or her audience and alters delivery accordingly. Successful interaction is a good tool to keep your prospects involved. Comfortable chairs should be positioned so that your prospects can see both you and the visuals that you will use.

Some characteristics that detract from effective verbal delivery:

● Use of unfamiliar terminology and acronyms
● Use of distractive phrases and non-words, such as 'OK', 'You know'.
● Speaking too quickly
● Speaking in a monotone
● Use of slang
● Lack of confidence
● Poor use of grammar
● Reading your visuals
● Addressing one person continuously with no eye contact with the rest of your prospects.

Even though your words may be exact and precise, they may not be particularly vivid. You can make them vivid by using gestures that visualize their meaning.

● **Eye contact.** It is to your advantage that you retain eye contact with your prospects. Typically, you might avoid it for reasons such as a fear of being turned down or rejected, or because you're too busy thinking on your feet. Eye contact reaffirms that you are focused on your prospects, and when you focus on you prospects, you are not focusing on your fear or on your own mental processes. The advantage is that your prospects pay attention to what you are saying.

● **Gestures.** Use large, descriptive gestures along with a big voice. Your words and hand movements must carry throughout the room. The benefits of descriptive hand movements and good vocal projection is that your message will be very vivid and clear.

● **Poise.** Stand straight, yet relaxed. Move around the platform, don't hang on the podium.

Your posture, foot placements and general movements – do they contribute to, or detract from, your making of an effective visual message?

● **Control.** Being aware of your audience will help to ensure that you have control of them. If they appear to be distracted or have lost interest, moving closer to them or using exaggerated gestures should regain their attention. Smile, as it will relax both you and your audience.

Some characteristics that detract from effective physical delivery include:

● Minimal eye contact
● Small, descriptive gestures as they are invariably accompanied by a small voice. Your prospects will neither be able to hear nor visualize your message.
● Distracting gestures
● Poor posture (slouching)
● Untidy dress sense
● Unsmiling attitude.

TIP 66 *The Percentages Game*

In my introduction, I spoke of percentages. If you take the three areas of selling – who you call on, what you talk to those people about and how you present your ideas to those same people – I know that you will immediately recognize where the percentages lie in the who and the what.

Who do you call on for the best percentage of success? A decision-maker or a non-decision-maker? Obviously, the decision-maker.

What do you talk to that person about: specific facts, problems and benefits or general facts, problems and benefits? Obviously, specific, because this is where the business persons interests truly lie.

But how do you present these facts and information? Verbally, or backed up with the use of various visual aids so that people can see what you are talking about? Again, the advantage of the second approach is obvious – yet there is a distinct reluctance by some salespeople to use visual aids. You will never be successful in closing those bigger deals unless you also master the use of presentations incorporating some form of visual aid. Generally, people comprehend: 11 per cent of what they hear, 32 per cent of what they see, 73 per cent of what they hear and see, and 90 per cent of what they hear, see and discuss.

There are bound to be occasions when you will be unable to call on that decision-maker and you will find yourself talking to people on general facts and problems, especially if you have gained little information on your account. But there are very few occasions when you cannot add to your percentage of success by using some form of visual aid to help you communicate your ideas.

An effective visual presentation is, very simply, a tool to visualize the highlights of your proposal and to provide you with a guide and prompt. In this way, you are helped in communicating your ideas, thereby increasing your likely percentage of selling success.

Some ingredients of an effective visual presentation are:

- *It must stimulate interest – from beginning to end:* if it is not interesting and does not relate to areas of prospect concern then your prospect has every right to curtail your presentation.
- *It must guide you:* moreover, it must guide you *logically*. It must stress the high points so that you can 'verbalize' the information you require and inspire two-way communication between you and your prospect. It will also prevent you from rambling too far off-track and help you to use your prospect's time more effectively.
- *It must be creative:* although you may not consider yourself a naturally creative person, the best visual presentations are personalized by the individual that uses them. Many creative resources are available to you – your manager, colleagues and support groups. Alternatively, trade journals and market research companies are excellent sources of additional and relevant information.
- *It must be concise:* if you are giving your

final proposal presentation (after a lengthy sales campaign), holding a six inch binder, your audience may be reluctant to let you start! On the other hand, a concise visual presentation ensures a receptive audience.

● *It must be specific:* your highest percentage of success comes from that specific information relating directly to your prospect. The more specific, the more effective. Where there are 'difficult' sections within the presentation, they should be visualized so that they will be more easily understood. Wording should be kept as simple as possible and should lead your prospect logically through your presentation.

Visuals are not a crutch, but a way of reinforcing your contact. They should be used whenever possible, whether in a one-to-one or group environment, as there is now substantial evidence to suggest that 75 per cent of what we store in our brains is stored visually. Confucius said, 'One picture is worth a thousand words'. The brain works at ten times the speed of speaking – adding significant content to any picture.

TIP 68 *Get Creative!*

Now that you have got your message right and added analogies, facts and figures, you can turn your attention to the creation of your visuals.

The three types of visuals most often used in business presentations are slides, foils and flipcharts. In addition, with the use of a Personal Computer, you can achieve a new dimension to presentations. You can create, edit and sequence pictures and then show them as your complete story, still applying the basic principles of visual creation.

Some general principles in the creation of effective visuals are:

● **Make them large.**
Lettering and pictures should be large enough to be seen from the back of the room with ease.

● **Make them simple.**
Your visuals should not be 'busy', but simple and easy to understand.

● **Use colour.**
Variety can easily be built into your visuals by the application of colour. Red draws the greatest notice and should be used to draw attention to an important figure or letter.

● **Words.**
When carefully selected for impact, words on your visuals can be very effective. But you should limit the

number – too many words force your prospect's attention away from you, the presenter.

● **Anticipation.** Too often, presenters show their visual aids and then proceed to explain what they mean! This is in contravention of the principles of using visual aids. They are what they say they are – an AID, not a REPLACEMENT.

● **Dramatize.** Bring your visuals to life by involving yourself in them. Do it by circling figures, drawing in the trend line as you mention it, writing in figures, and using colours.

● **Your audience.** There are two things to remember when relating to your audience: they are the ones to receive your message and your eyes must be focused on them and not on your visuals; your visuals must be able to be seen, with ease, by everyone in your audience.

● **Your position.** The best place for you to stand is to the left of the screen (or to the right, as your audiences looks at you).

As the eye travels naturally from left to right, and since you want the natural eye contact of your prospects on you, you should stand where your prospects' eyes will naturally travel to you.

● **Pictures.**

We are all visual beings. We think in pictures. We dream in pictures. Any subject can be visualized into pictures when you apply your imagination. Pictures are the key to opening the mind of your audience to an understanding of your message.

● **Use of notes.**

Your visuals themselves are an important part of the note process, but you often forget that verbal bridge that you intended to use from one visual to another. To jog your memory, keep a brief synopsis of each of your visuals, enabling you to recall the immediate, salient points.

TIP 69 *Make Your Choice*

There are advantages and disadvantages to each of your media choices: slides, foils, flipcharts and personal computer-based visuals.

Slides
- Advantages:
  - Durability
  - Flexibility
  - Large or small audience
  - Ability to visualize concepts.

- Disadvantages:
  - Cost of material
  - Production time
  - Audience can become passive in darkened room
  - Not easily revised
  - Dependent on operable slide projector
  - Flexibility can be lost because the sequence of slides is predetermined and it is difficult to re-sequence during the actual presentation.

Foils
If you were asked what you found annoying about foils when you are *in an audience*, the chances are that you would answer as follows: 'Too many foils, too much material on foils, can't read foils, speaker fumbles with order of foils'.

If you were asked what you found difficult about foils *when you were a presenter*, the chances are you might answer: Where to put them, when to put them up, when to take them down, hard to read.

It is interesting that, as a presenter, you focus on the *skills* of using foils, while being asked as a member of the audience, you focus on the *context*.

● Advantages:
- They can be used to present effectively to an audience of up to 50 people
- They can be revised
- As they are typically produced from a typed or printed page, handouts can be produced with ease
- Sequence can be changed during your presentation
- Inexpensive
- Maintenance of eye contact possible (no darkened room).

● Disadvantages:
- Dependent on operable foil projector
- Movement is restricted
- Cannot effectively address as large an audience as with slides.

Always keep foils simple – ten lines maximum, with one main message per foil. Use indented sub-headings, and make them clear – three colours maximum. Make them *visual* by using simple graphic design, diagrams and symbols.

Make Your Choice

Flip charts

Most presenters today prefer to use flipcharts for recording input only. They are good visual devices for summarizing statements. Some general recommendations for using flip charts are:

- Talk to your audience, not to the flipchart. Maintain eye contact.
- Write large so that your audience can read the information.
- Use coloured pens to emphasize ideas or categorize the information
- Point to items on your flipcharts as you mention them.

Using flipcharts in the above professional manner helps you to convince your audience that you are taking their input seriously.

- Advantages:
  - Ability to tailor
  - No audiovisual equipment necessary
  - Relatively portable
  - Flexible format
  - Easy to prepare.

- Disadvantages:
  - There are limits to the size of audience that can effectively be addressed
  - Not very durable
  - Requires good printing/difficult to main-

tain high quality
- Takes time
- Require a flip chart stand.

Personal computer-based visuals
The use of the Personal Computer helps you to achieve outstanding results by using software that enables you to create, edit and sequence pictures and text, showing them as a complete story.

- Advantages:
  - Durable
  - Flexible
  - Portable (diskette)
  - Can be presented to both large and small audiences
  - Visualizes well/exciting
  - Relatively simple revision.

- Disadvantages:
  - Revision can be cumbersome for a complex presentation
  - Lose flexibility once presentation starts. Very difficult to change order
  - Need skilled and knowledgeable technician.

Handouts
Only use a handout if your audience really needs more information than you can easily present verbally or on a foil. While it is easy to

produce a handout from your foil presentation,
a good foil is not necessarily a good handout.
Use handouts for:

● Supplementary information
● Extremely complex information
● Reinforcing future desired actions
● Ammunition, in anticipation of serious
  doubts from your audience.

TIP 70

Who Side-Tracked you Last?

You have probably had the experience of being side-tracked by your audience during a presentation. Their input is often both unexpected and unfocused. You find yourself covering a wide range of topics in an attempt to respond. You can further detract from your presentation by matching an emotional question with an emotional response. In managing your audience, there are two sets of skills involved:

- **Receptive.** The message that you are communicating must be flexible enough to accept input from your audience. As a result, you open up to your audience's views, facilitate audience involvement and accept all audience input. But you direct the process by asking good questions and by being a good listener. You make good use of eye contact, maintaining rapport with your audience. To record and summarize your audience's input, you make use of flipcharts.
- **Assertive.** You take a firm line and drive home the message. You press your point. You control and direct audience participation. You stress positives and minimize negatives. You promote your own content. You will

break eye contact with a questioner and forcefully use your body language. To be assertive and retain total credibility takes great audience management skills.

- When a member of your audience asks a question, listen for the issue and rephrase to clarify
- Respond with a brief and forceful answer, leaving no room for additional input
- Ensure that you connect your answer back to your main message.

STEP THIRTEEN

SUCCESSFUL SEMINARS

TIP 71

Spread the Word

To sell effectively in any environment, including that of the large account, you need the means to put over a clear sales message to groups of prospects. In the case of the large account, for example, this could be a specific department, or to a group of middle or senior management. By running a business meeting or seminar, specially tailored to your prospect's areas of interest, you create that unrivalled opportunity to explain 'up-front' what your company stands for and outline your solutions and services. Prospects can make an initial evaluation of you as a company. Expertly handled, seminars within your large account will provide you with detailed feedback on your account's real needs and attitudes, valuable input to your marketing planning. Often, these large account groups may not be your normal contacts within the account; but information is power and you should take every opportunity to elicit whatever you can.

Your prospects also benefit from a well-organized seminar. They are provided with sound information in their sphere of interest with a chance to discuss their overall needs, all of which may be difficult to get in other ways.

For greatest effect, the seminar must address a specific business area. Not only is this more attractive to the audience than a general meeting, but it also enables you to structure your event for the highest levels of presentation.

The way you organize your event reflects just

as much on the quality and capability of your company as any other activity you undertake. Planning and attention to detail are, by far, the most important ingredients.

TIP 72 *It's That Planning Again!*

Aim for simplicity in all your arrangements. Not only is there less to go wrong but it can also appear more professional.

Objectives

Success will depend on two factors: setting realistic goals and planning to meet those goals. For instance, you must establish what it is that you are trying to achieve from this seminar. This may sound obvious, but if you identify a clear, overall objective, you can determine whether each individual part of your seminar contributes to the whole. Focus on one objective – audience confusion progresses at an accelerated rate when more than one idea is presented. Two ideas are more than twice as difficult to understand as one clearly stated.

Measure each aspect of your seminar against the question, 'Does this help me achieve my aims for the day?' The result will be a well-integrated programme with a strong message. Here are some questions to assist you in defining your objectives:

- What are your marketing objectives for your seminar?
- How will these objectives help you hold or increase your share of sales?
- What new and existing concepts, solutions, features and services to be included?
- What will be their order of importance in relation to the audience invited?

● What is the description of these concepts and solutions in terms of function, benefit and price?
● What sales volumes and revenue are forecast by solution or service, by industry, by geographic area? Or, by individual departments, for example, if you were running a set of seminars in a large account?
● What is your company's current status in these areas?
● Who will be the key people at your seminar? What are their characteristics?
● What are their buying habits, preferences and needs? Are these changing?
● Where is demand increasing? Where is it declining?
● Why should your prospects buy from you rather than your competitors?
● What are your competitors' strengths, weaknesses and trends?
● What sales aids should you be using?

Whatever your objectives, once you've set them by understanding your purpose in running your seminar, be realistic – set them within reason. This means, don't try too hard. There are four 'musts' in setting your objectives:

● *Objectives must have a numerical projection of the expected results:* you must have a target in order to be committed to hitting it. They should, therefore, be stated precisely

and in measurable form.
- *They should be practical:* restrict them to important results.
- *They should be difficult, but attainable.*
- *They must be exciting.*
- *They must be big:* you can't get excited about mediocrity. But you can get excited about getting ahead . . . being more successful.

Audience
To meet their expectations of the day, it's important to know your audience's interests, their level of expertise and why they have accepted your invitation. It helps to define your audience at the start by deciding who should be invited. Your own prospects? If so, you already know a little about them. Specific industry? Relate your presentations precisely to their interest areas. Individual departments of your large accounts? Again, you already know a little about them. How many? This will be decided by the form and content of your programme. For example, if you are holding a 'workshop', you won't aim for a huge audience in theatre-style seating!

When?
Set the date well in advance. Check that there are no conflicting events and it's not a peak workload period.

Where?
Whether you choose the traditional 'hotel' or go for something more off-beat, you need to consider factors such as access, parking, catering, electrical supply and so on. If you are using your prospect's premises, then your location decision is made easy, although there are some factors that you will want to consider. The following list will help you determine what you need to think about when taking an outside location.

● Proximity of your location to your target prospects
● Image you are trying to project
● Space. Are there separate facilities for both coffee and a buffet lunch?
● Electrical power – sufficient outlets?
● Sufficient catering staff for coffee/buffet lunch?
● Adequate parking? Is a map available?
● How easy is access by public transport?
● How good are the acoustics?
● Equipment. Most locations offering seminar facilities provide required items, such as overhead projectors, screens etc
● Access for your equipment
● Telephones. Are there facilities for urgent messages?
● Lighting. Are there dimmers, easy controls?
● Heating/air conditioning?
● Seating. Quantity and comfort?

- Noise. Are there other functions running at the same time? Is there any building work in progress?
- Stage/podium. Do you need either?
- Washrooms. Are they adequate and convenient?
- Are there photocopying facilities and typing services?
- Communications. Can you have a separate, dedicated telephone line?
- Can you arrange early access to the location for set-up?
- Is there a conference/seminar manager/manageress and will he/she be on duty?
- Is the location clearly signposted?
- Is there a special registration or reception area?
- Is there a place to take coats?

Finance

No doubt you will have a budget, or at least an idea of how much you can spend on the event. Establish which costs are fixed, which are variable. Also, what costs are involved should you decide to cancel? Try to foresee, and budget for, variations such as larger or smaller numbers.

Organization

Who has overall responsibility? Decide at the start, to avoid confusion at a later date. Make arrangements for any additional secretarial support and reception help you may need.

Speakers

Nominate a 'host' – who may be you or another speaker – to welcome your audience, explain the format and introduce other speakers. Vary your speakers to keep audience interest high.

To add that convincing note to your efforts, involve customers as guest speakers wherever possible. Any audience is particularly impressed when they hear from someone in their own industry or using similar applications. Their experiences and successes will be well-accepted.

Publicity

How will you invite people? An invitation card? A direct marketing letter? By telephone? A combination? Decide according to the number of people that you hope will attend.

Overall objectives

Check once more that the concept you have mapped out for your seminar supports your original objectives which, in turn, support your marketing plan. Every seminar presentation is a sales opportunity and should be structured as a selling vehicle.

The aim of your invitation is to generate a response that leads to attendance, so make sure that your invitation spells out clearly WHAT the objective of your event is, WHERE and WHEN it will be held, and HOW attendees will benefit. The easier you make it for people to reply, the more replies you will receive. Make the invitation enticing and understandable. Use a pre-printed reply form or reply-paid card and give one point of contact, preferably a name and telephone number. Address the letter or invitation personally, if possible, and keep it simple. Avoid old English such as, 'contact the undersigned', that distance you from your prospects.

When you have sent out your invitations, the manner in which you follow them up can dramatically affect your eventual attendance figures. Log all responses carefully. Positive responses should be sent an immediate confirmation. Two days before your seminar, call your attendees as a reminder, or confirmation, of their attendance. If your initial invitation is refused, you can still use the 'contact' of those refusals to build for the future. Send a response saying you were sorry to learn that they could not attend.

If you receive no response at all to your invitation, you should use the telephone as a powerful marketing tool. Acceptances gained this way should, again, be confirmed immediately by letter, underlining your commitment and your professionalism.

Remember in particular to:

● Make sure that one person is made responsible for keeping track of acceptances and for listing the attendees
● Plan carefully to avoid too many acceptances, which can be as disappointing for your seminar as too few. If your event *is* oversubscribed, you may be able to split it into morning and afternoon sessions or run a second event on the following day
● Invite 'named' contacts wherever possible
● Confirm attendance, by telephone, two days before your seminar
● Acknowledge all responses, positive or negative, and you will achieve a high attendance more easily as well as demonstrating your professionalism.

TIP 74 *It's Detail that Counts*

The most successful seminars appear to move effortlessly between one session and the next. But this is always the result of careful, detailed planning – well before the seminar date.

Ensure that each of your staff involved in the seminar is responsible for a particular part of the preparation and that each continually reports on progress to the overall seminar co-ordinator.

Plan your agenda carefully. Prepare each presentation according to the time allotted and its place in the day's events. If you are running a large seminar, you should arrange for a 'dress rehearsal'. Check that your location allows you easy access for this full rehearsal.

Make sure that any demonstration session has also been well-rehearsed, with a competent speaker and demonstrator. Inexpertly handled, demonstrations can be both confusing and boring.

Before the event, sit in every seat, making sure that you can see and read your charts/foils. Carry out the same checks on microphones and any remote control devices.

Tip *75* *On the Day*

Your opening remarks are important. They make an enduring first impression on your prospects and they set the tone for the day. Your audience has given up time to attend, so will certainly listen, at least to the beginning. Don't let this chance pass you by!

First, introduce yourself and everyone taking part. Your own staff should be clearly identified. Relax your audience by explaining the comfort items (locations of toilets and telephones, arrangements that have been made to take messages and what time the breaks will be). Then, thank them for being there. Make it clear that you recognize that they've made an investment of time to attend, (not even free seminars are really 'free').

Show the agenda, even if you have sent it previously. It helps to show a clear-cut agenda so that the breaks and conclusion times are clear. Keeping to this agenda will add to your confident, professional image.

Pitch your talk for the audience, not for your subject-matter. Although you may cover the same subject in several seminars, each will be different because each audience and its interests will be different. Sometimes, when you are deeply involved in detailed arrangements and rehearsals, it's hard to remember that the seminar is only there for the attendees – not vice versa!

Try to sense how your audience is responding. Ask questions. Encourage a certain amount of interaction – it will give you a measure of how things are going and keeps the audience alert and involved. When a member of the audience asks a question, repeat it to make sure that everyone has heard it. Then address your answer to everyone, not just the individual.

Use analogies in your presentation. Make it fun to be there – a sense of humour can enliven even a mundane subject, yet still reinforce a strong point at the same time.

Limit your use of foils and other visual aids. Over-reliance on them can make a presentation very stilted. If it's worth saying, say it to the audience. Don't be afraid of silences – you can use them to emphasize a point or to let your audience absorb an idea while you change foils or check your notes.

Try to speak as you would in normal conversation, with inflections and pauses, rather than speaking non-stop in a monotone. And try to address yourself to everyone in turn while you are talking – make sure that you don't concentrate only on the people nearest to you. Talk to someone all of the time; talk to everyone some of the time.

When you're presenting at a seminar, you're selling. You're not only selling your solutions and/or services, you're selling your company, yourself and your seminar's benefits to the attendees. One of your first selling jobs of the day is to sell the attendee on the idea of wanting to listen to what you have to say. You must start with the assumption that nobody wants to be there, or to stay – this challenge provides a good basis for developing the content of your presentation.

People like to be involved. Involve your audience by inviting their reactions to your topics (using names if you can). Don't concentrate on the one or two more out-going members of the audience, but draw in others too. It's important for people to feel that they are participating, rather than being lectured to. As concentration only lasts for about 45 minutes, arrange for presentations to change regularly.

People can't absorb too much complex information. It helps to restate key points. Remember the old adage: *tell them what you're going to tell them; tell them; tell them what you've told them.*

There are many ways in which your staff can contribute. By listening to comments, talking to prospects during the breaks and helping with questions, they can gain valuable feedback on audience reaction. This broadens their experience in dealing with prospects and provides useful guidance for your next seminar.

It's human nature not to comment or ask questions in an unfamiliar group. You may well find that it is difficult to draw out your audience when together. Your participants will feel more relaxed when they have had a chance to get to know people a little, over lunch or coffee. Make use of these informal breaks to discuss ideas, problems and queries.

It's your home ground (even if it's not your premises) so don't allow your guests to feel isolated or stand neglected in a group. In their eyes, you and your staff are the experts. Get them talking. Ask them questions.

TIP 76 *The Follow-up*

The follow-up is the crucial phase in your marketing programme. At the end of your seminar, each prospect should feel sufficiently informed and encouraged to make a decision about your company and its offerings. You and your staff should be able to qualify each prospect as to the likelihood of their purchasing, recommending or influencing the purchase of your product/services.

Seminar participants will eventually fall into one or two types: buyers and non-buyers. Your seminar was an effort to change prospects into those buyers, recommenders or influencers (all of whom can be termed 'buyers'). Now, you must isolate them and concentrate on them, providing any additional information they might need. For the non-buyers, there must also be a positive plan, including remaining in contact and maintaining the 'conversation' through other invitations to future seminars.

Take advantage of the awareness that your seminar has generated and commit those prospects to do business with your company. Don't delay your follow-up. The enthusiasm that you raised will fade in a few days. Make that telephone call aimed at obtaining that appointment. Your prospects expect it. It emphasizes the organized, professional approach of your company and shows you care whether your prospects buy, recommend or influence.

Example of a Seminar Assessment Form

Thank you for attending the . . . . seminar. We hope that you found the day both useful and interesting.

It would be appreciated if you would complete this form so that we can assess your observations of the content, value and overall presentation of this seminar.

Key: E = Excellent VG = Very Good S = Satisfactory P = Poor

Tick as appropriate:

Module name	Content				Presentation			
	E	VG	S	P	E	VG	S	P
Introduction	—	—	—	—	—	—	—	—
Module X	—	—	—	—	—	—	—	—
Module Y	—	—	—	—	—	—	—	—
Module Z	—	—	—	—	—	—	—	—
Q and A	—	—	—	—	—	—	—	—
Summary	—	—	—	—	—	—	—	—
Location	—	—	—	—	—	—	—	—
Overall value	—	—	—	—	—	—	—	—

I would like further information on: . . . .
I would like to discuss my requirements . . . .
I would like to place an order with you . . . .

Name . . . . Title . . . .
Company . . . .
Address . . . .
. . . .
. . . .
Postal Code . . . . Telephone . . . .

Thank you for taking the time to complete this form. It will allow us to take appropriate steps in future seminars and any action as requested by yourselves. Please hand this form to the receptionist.

TIP 78 *Was It Worth It?*

At the time of your seminar, you and your staff are probably too tense and too closely involved to judge the event objectively. There is a temptation simply to be enthusiastic about the event's success and analyze it no further.

However, you need to take a long, cool look at the success and failure of each part of your seminar. Using the assessment form on page 00, list the average results by section, together with any audience comments for improvement. It's a good idea to give the same form to your staff who were present at the time. Their internal view is often even sharper and more objective than your prospect's views. Compare the two – the differences will be as interesting as the similarities.

Here are some questions to ask yourself about the day:

- Did it meet my objectives?
- Was it within budget?
- Were the details properly planned?
- Was the location right?
- Did we get the right level of attendance?
- Did we run on time?
- Was the introduction too long/too short?
- Did we handle the Q and A session correctly?
- Were all the visual aids relevant?
- How well did our speakers perform?
- Was the demonstration (if any) smooth and professional?
- Was there enough food and coffee?

- Did all the acceptances arrive? If not, why not?
- Did we have enough equipment and of the right type?
- Would we do it the same way next time?

Only when you have completed your reviews of the whole event – honestly – can you congratulate yourself, if it proved successful. But the event is only part of it. If you generate no sales revenue from the attendant prospects and their companies, then your event has been a singular failure!

Suggested timetable of events

	Who	Target Date	Complete
Six months before			
Announce seminar plans	_____	_____	_____
Discuss objectives (attendance/sales)	_____	_____	_____
Book location	_____	_____	_____
Four weeks before			
Confirm seminar date(s). Time.	_____	_____	_____
Prepare agenda	_____	_____	_____
Prepare presentations	_____	_____	_____
Invite guest speakers (if using)	_____	_____	_____
Prepare demonstration (if any)	_____	_____	_____
Develop invitation list	_____	_____	_____
Prepare invitation/ letter	_____	_____	_____
Prepare attendance letter	_____	_____	_____
Prepare follow-up letters	_____	_____	_____
Check administrative support	_____	_____	_____
Check availability of demonstration units (if any)	_____	_____	_____
Arrange technical/			

Your Timetable

	Who	Target Date	Complete
Arrange technical/ engineering support (if required)	_____	_____	_____
Prepare handout material	_____	_____	_____
Three weeks before			
Begin invitation/letter/ phone	_____	_____	_____
Review seminar plan/ agenda	_____	_____	_____
Confirm guest speakers	_____	_____	_____
Two weeks before			
Mail 'accept' response letter	_____	_____	_____
Mail 'sorry you can't make it' letter	_____	_____	_____
Reserve necessary equipment	_____	_____	_____
Review progress with staff	_____	_____	_____
One week before			
Begin attendance assurance (telephone)	_____	_____	_____
Practise presentations	_____	_____	_____
Practise demonstrations	_____	_____	_____
Assemble visuals	_____	_____	_____
Assemble handouts	_____	_____	_____

Your Timetable

	Who	Target Date	Com- plete
Organize reception/ registration	____	____	____
Order refreshments (quantity)	____	____	____
Check off acceptances	____	____	____
Two days before			
List confirmed attendees	____	____	____
Prepare name badges/ tags	____	____	____
Assemble total presentation, handouts and demonstration material	____	____	____
One day before			
Full rehearsal	____	____	____
Set up all facilities (if possible)	____	____	____
Check equipment	____	____	____
Check direction signs (hotel lobby)	____	____	____
Confirm refreshments	____	____	____
Reconfirm guest speakers	____	____	____
Contingency plan	____	____	____
Seminar day			
Personnel arrive at least one hour early	____	____	____

Your Timetable

	Who	Target Date	Com- plete
Review agenda with personnel	____	____	____
Ensure refreshments are set up	____	____	____
Check facilities and equipment	____	____	____
Set up attendee handouts/reception	____	____	____
Final check on direction signs	____	____	____
Register attendees	____	____	____
Seminar performance			
Seminar host/overview	____	____	____
Welcome/mood setting	____	____	____
Seminar presentations	____	____	____
Equipment demonstration (if any)	____	____	____
Q and A session	____	____	____
Evaluate forms	____	____	____
Conclusion	____	____	____
One day after			
Start follow-up campaign	____	____	____
Telephone for appointments	____	____	____
Send follow-up letters	____	____	____
Evaluate success/ failure of seminar	____	____	____

Your Timetable

	Who	Target Date	Complete
Tracking system for attendees	___	___	___
On-going Keep staff informed of successes	___	___	___

STEP FOURTEEN

YOU CAN'T ESCAPE THE ASSESSMENT!

TIP *80* *Check out Yourself*

Skills self-assessment – how good are you?
   5 = Expert, can teach others
   4 = Self-sufficient
   3 = Satisfactory
   2 = Needs management assistant
   1 = Awareness only
N/A = Not applicable

	Present Rating
1) *Assessing key account sales potential and setting objectives*	
Analyzing sales and account information	5 4 3 2 1 N/A
Setting realistic sales objectives	5 4 3 2 1 N/A
Setting measurable sales objectives	5 4 3 2 1 N/A
Identifying high potential	5 4 3 2 1 N/A
Overall rating in this area	5 4 3 2 1 N/A
2) *Managing the key account*	
Maintain accurate account records	5 4 3 2 1 N/A
Developing an account plan as a result of a formal planning session	5 4 3 2 1 N/A
Preparation for sales calls	5 4 3 2 1 N/A
Implementing the account plan overall	5 4 3 2 1 N/A

Present Rating

Budgeting and controlling
   expenses   5 4 3 2 1 N/A
Handling administrative
   responsibilities   5 4 3 2 1 N/A
Overall rating in this area 5 4 3 2 1 N/A

3) *Selling*
Maintaining relationships
   with decision-makers
   in your accounts 5 4 3 2 1 N/A
Establishing productive
   relationships with your
   customers and staff 5 4 3 2 1 N/A
Identifying and
   confirming needs 5 4 3 2 1 N/A
Making effective sales
   presentations 5 4 3 2 1 N/A
Handling objections and
   gaining commitment 5 4 3 2 1 N/A
Effective implementation
   of marketing
   programmes 5 4 3 2 1 N/A
Financial justification
   skills 5 4 3 2 1 N/A
Key account development 5 4 3 2 1 N/A
Overall rating in this area 5 4 3 2 1 N/A

4) *Communicating and
maintaining effective
working relationships*

	Present Rating
Developing productive relationships with appropriate staffs	5 4 3 2 1 N/A
Contributing to a strong account team effort	5 4 3 2 1 N/A
Overall rating in this area	5 4 3 2 1 N/A

5) *Managing self-development/acquiring product and service knowledge*

Gaining/maintaining product/service knowledge	5 4 3 2 1 N/A
Participating in training/ professional development programmes	5 4 3 2 1 N/A
Evaluating and improving job skills	5 4 3 2 1 N/A
Managing your career development	5 4 3 2 1 N/A
Overall rating in this area	5 4 3 2 1 N/A

6) *Total job skills rating*   5 4 3 2 1 N/A